Japanese Bitcoin Law

Karl-Friedrich Lenz

Copyright © 2014 Karl-Friedrich Lenz
License:
Creative Commons Attribution-NonCommercial 3.0 Unported

Available as a FREE PDF file at k-lenz.de/btcjapan.
ISBN: **1502353032**
ISBN-13: **978-1502353030**

CONTENTS

Acknowledgments	i
Introduction	1
Chapter 1: General Issues	8
Chapter 2: Licensing and Oversight	62
Chapter 3: Trading Rules	154
Chapter 4: Tax Law and Criminal Law	174

ACKNOWLEDGMENTS

Thanks go to Zoë Markham for the fast turnaround on the editing of this project, and to Kolin Burges and Jon Southurst for the permission to use the photo on the cover of this book.
.

INTRODUCTION

I wanted to know how Japanese law relates to bitcoin exchanges like MtGox, and to the Bitcoin network in general. The best way for me to find out was to write this short book.

I am not going to explain here what Bitcoin is[1]. Or who MtGox is[2]. This book is for people who already know that much.

Why would I be interested in such a question?

By a weird coincidence, I was involved in some of the protests going on at the MtGox office in January and February 2014. Two threads on Reddit about these protests got quite a lot of attention and comments.

One of them was about a guy from Australia who flew in spending more than 16 hours on the road just to talk to someone from MtGox in person. I have talked to him and know his name, but I won't mention it here, since he asked me not to disclose that particular detail.

---

[1] See the "Bitcoin" Wikipedia article at en.wikipedia.org/wiki/Bitcoin.
[2] See the "MtGox" Wikipedia article at en.wikipedia.org/wiki/MtGox.

He posted a report about his adventure on Reddit in this thread.[3] Which got a score of over 1300 upvotes and over 600 comments.

As I mentioned in that thread[4], I was walking from my university over to the weekly Bitcoin Meetup in Shibuya. Since the MtGox office is located on my way there, I happened to notice this protester standing there with a sign. I thought he might be interested in joining the Meetup, so I approached him and told him that there was a Bitcoin Meetup scheduled close by. And asked if he would be interested in attending.

He was. So we walked over there together and discussed his protest on the way.

After he returned to Australia, a second guy came over from London the next week. He had seen my post at Reddit and contacted me. We ended up having lunch together, joined by a journalist from the Wall Street Journal.

He succeeded in confronting the CEO of MtGox, Mark Karpeles, and getting that confrontation on video[5]. The Wall Street Journal

---

[3] k-lenz.de/btc001.

[4] k-lenz.de/btc002.

[5] k-lenz.de/btc003.

reported on the protest[6]. Coindesk reported as well[7].

The picture on the cover of this book is of him standing in a snowstorm protesting.

I met some other people involved as well. So I got a pretty good picture of what was going on.

Very briefly: The MtGox exchange had suspended withdrawals of bitcoins, allegedly for a technical reason. They had already just about stopped withdrawals of actual money before. And on top of that, they were stonewalling people.

There was no actual money coming out, no bitcoins coming out, and no information coming out.

And then they moved out of their office space and gave a "virtual office" address instead.

I wonder what the Japanese Prime Minister would do with a bank that suspended withdrawals of actual money because they couldn't be bothered to keep their computer code up to date. And that on top of that refused to talk to journalists, refused to talk to large depositors, and did not disclose their financial statements. And on top of <u>that</u> closed all of their branches to hide behind a post box virtual office address. No one would know about the financial

---

[6] k-lenz.de/btc004.
[7] k-lenz.de/btc005.

health of such a bank.

Might the Prime Minister be inclined to revoke the license of such a bank?

Might he be inclined to do so if he saw press reports of people flying in from overseas to protest the sorry state of Japanese banking regulation?

Might he want to revoke the banking license of MtGox?

Wait a minute.

It's impossible to revoke the banking license of MtGox. They don't have one in the first place.

It's also impossible to damage their reputation as an honest bitcoin exchange at this point (23 February 2014). They don't have any such reputation left in the first place. And actually, a couple of days after I wrote the sentence above, MtGox announced that they had lost hundreds of millions of dollars in bitcoins to "hackers" and that they are filing for "civil rehabilitation".

So that leads to the interesting question: Would MtGox have needed a banking license for what they were doing?

I am going to spend some time in the first chapter discussing exactly that question in some detail.

But this book is only partly about the MtGox problem. They may get shut down by the Japanese regulators. Mark Karpeles may be prosecuted in criminal court for violation of the Japanese Banking Act or other relevant statutes.

I don't care either way if that happens. What I care about is finding out what the law says right now in Japan.

One motive for this is that eventually people will want to set up other bitcoin exchanges in Japan. They will need to know what the legal requirements for such an exchange are.

One other motive is the simple fact that I enjoy researching and writing about law.

And bitcoin (the unit of currency) and Bitcoin (the network and the protocol) are a major innovation, comparable to the personal computer and the Internet.

A note on spelling. In this book, I consistently use the spelling "Bitcoin" (capital B) when talking about the Bitcoin network or the Bitcoin protocol, or other parts of the Bitcoin infrastructure like miners, payment processors, or online wallets. In contrast, I use the spelling "bitcoin" (small b) when talking about the units of currency allowed on that network.

I think this difference is important. One analogy would be services like Twitter or Youtube and the Internet. The Internet is the protocol and the network, and Twitter and Youtube are built on top of it. In the same way, bitcoins move over the Bitcoin network.

This is, in my opinion, the way to give an objective value for individual bitcoins. That value depends on the strength of the underlying infrastructure. And of course on the number of users (network effect). Both of these are growing exponentially, which means that eventually the price of individual bitcoins will do so as well. It has grown in average by a factor of 10 each year for the past couple of years, and as long as the exponential growth of the Bitcoin network keeps up, that growth will continue for another couple of years.

Before starting, I need to write a couple of lines of disclosure.

I am personally a customer of MtGox, with about half a bitcoin and some small change stuck at the exchange at the time of this writing. That means I do have a small amount of money at stake personally here. But I think it is safe to say that this does not influence my judgment in any way.

I also had the pleasure of talking to all three people protesting at the MtGox office directly. Part of my motivation comes from a desire to make sure this kind of thing doesn't become necessary again.

In contrast, I have attempted repeatedly to talk to MtGox, but have had no success. They are ignoring me, just like most everyone else.

I have been offered a consulting fee for discussing legal questions with one individual. I have not accepted that, nor have I accepted any consulting fee from anyone else in this matter, and I have no plans to do so in the future. I am writing this only as a public service. And, of course, because I think that this is a fascinating topic.

So let's get on with this show.

CHAPTER 1: GENERAL ISSUES

I. Bitcoin and Law

Some people involved with the Bitcoin protocol have a low opinion of law and government. They like the peer-to-peer nature of Bitcoin. Some have high hopes that the Bitcoin network will get rid of governments and laws altogether.

For example, Roger Ver donated in 2013 bitcoins worth more than one million dollars at the time to an organization. He talks about that donation in a Youtube video released in November 2013[8]. He donated the money to the FEE (Foundation for Economic Education) [9], citing their work in promoting the work of "intellectual giants" like Murray Rothbard[10].

Looking at the Wikipedia article on this intellectual giant, I find he advocated for ideas like "selling rights to children in a free market" (e.g. treating your child as an object of property, a slave), "enslavement of thieves to the victim", and "torturing

---

[8] k-lenz.de/btc053.
[9] www.fee.org/.
[10] en.wikipedia.org/wiki/Murray_Rothbard.

suspects of crime".

I think it is safe to say that all of these ideas are fringe minority loser positions in all civilized countries. They are incompatible with basic human rights guarantees as well. Any country in the EU adopting any of these proposals would find itself booted out of the European Union for human rights violations, as well it should.

In contrast, these ideas of rejecting government and law are not fringe minority loser positions when one restricts the voters to people already using bitcoins and advocating for the Bitcoin protocol. If one reads the Bitcoin discussions at Reddit, there are quite a lot of people who would support positions close to Roger Ver.

I think this is a problem. I want the Bitcoin protocol to be as successful as the Internet. I want it to go mainstream. That's impossible if it is joined at the hip with fringe minority loser political positions.

Fortunately, the Bitcoin protocol as such is completely neutral on these questions. Nothing in the protocol requires supporting slavery and torture.

And fortunately, the more extreme "libertarian[11]" Bitcoin supporters are more and more

---

[11] en.wikipedia.org/wiki/Libertarianism.

crowded out by investors from Wall Street. It is true that in the early days of the Bitcoin protocol, when 10,000 bitcoins would only buy you two pizzas, this fringe loser minority position had a strong influence. But this naturally changes as a larger part of the population starts using bitcoins. You can't expect to get Bitcoin mainstream and still keep a majority for your positions that are in a minority within the general population.

It is still true that getting the Bitcoin network to mainstream will, all things remaining equal, lead to a massive gain in economic freedom from regulation.

The Internet has made it possible for everyone to post videos to Youtube, like the video by Roger Ver I mentioned above. Before the Internet, you needed to be working for a television station to do that. Now everybody has that power.

The Internet has made it possible for everyone to write a novel and have it published at Createspace the next day. Before the Internet, you needed to write hundreds of query letters to publishers to get your novel out. Even Rowling's first "Harry Potter" book was rejected repeatedly. Now, those days are gone. Authors that are independent from legacy publishers are starting to make money from their efforts[12].

The Internet has made it possible for everyone to publish their opinion on a blog. Before the Internet, you needed to work at a newspaper to get the chance to reach an audience with your written articles.

All these examples show that the Internet was a great leap ahead for the freedom of speech. That's because the Internet is much more effective, and therefore much cheaper to use, than traditional media.

In exactly the same way, the Bitcoin protocol is much more effective, and therefore much cheaper to use, than the traditional financial system. And it will lead to much more economic freedom for everyone on the planet once it becomes mainstream.

I am happy about that. While I don't agree with the more radical "libertarian" ideas, I agree with the idea that law and regulations should respect the liberty of individuals. Actually, human rights protecting economic freedoms, like the freedom to choose one's profession or the guarantee of property against state expropriation, will be enhanced by the Bitcoin protocol, just like the Internet has enhanced freedom of speech.

---

[12] See this survey at authorearnings.com k-lenz.de/btc054.

But getting Bitcoin to mainstream will certainly not mean getting rid of governments and laws altogether. Thinking otherwise is similar to the illusion some people twenty years ago had that the Internet would get rid of governments and laws.

Actually, even if you happen to think that governments and laws should not exist, as a matter of fact, they do. And governments will enforce their laws even against people who don't like that fact.

For example, the position of rejecting all States and all laws obviously means opposing laws against producing, distributing, and possessing child porn. If there is no State and no law, obviously there will be no law against child porn either. But the expectation that the Internet would lead to a child porn producer's paradise where these laws suddenly disappear or lose all their effectiveness has not materialized. The FBI knows a thing or two about how to break tools like the Tor network. They just did so[13] by distributing malware on some child porn darknet websites.

So even if you are some kind of anarchist, at least as long as the Bitcoin network has not yet succeeded in its mission to get rid of governments

---

[13] Kashmir Hill, The Tech War On Child Porn Is Not Limited To Google Scanning Gmail, August 5 2014 blog post, k-lenz.de/btc104.

and laws, you would be well advised to find out what the law says about Bitcoin.

Right now, in most jurisdictions, there is no specific Bitcoin law. Just as around 1995 there was no specific Internet law. That will change. Eventually politicians are going to figure out what a revolutionary new technology Bitcoin is. It is, put very briefly, adding the ability to make payments to the peer-to-peer Internet. Of course there will be Bitcoin specific regulation eventually, just as there was Internet specific regulation eventually.

But until that happens, existing laws will be applied to the Bitcoin network. If someone steals a paper wallet, he will be accused and sentenced for theft. There is no need for a new statute in that case. If someone does not steal the paper wallet, but takes a picture of the private key with his mobile phone instead, that's a case where one would need to discuss if the existing theft statute applies. I will do so below.

But anyway, existing laws apply to the Bitcoin network even if they were not enacted with that network in mind.

To conclude this rather abstract section, let's discuss one very controversial point.

I have made a so called "vanity address". That address is published on my blog. It starts with the string 1KfLenzKgDW". I have done this for several reasons.

One is that this gives me the ability to use this Bitcoin address as a means of signing an online version of one of my books. I can create a virtual autograph. I posted in some detail [14] about this particular idea on my blog last year.

A big company like Coca-Cola might want to have a Bitcoin address in the format "1CocaCoLa". Or maybe add something like "777" for "1CocaCoLa777" (a long vanity address that requires considerable resources to find).

If it is known and easily proved to anyone caring to check that this address is indeed owned by Coca-Cola, then any payments to that address come with an instant receipt incorporated in the blockchain. And it would be close to impossible to divert any Bitcoin payment to some other address, since finding another address with the correct format would be very expensive, which would be enough to discourage anybody from trying this for amounts worth less than is necessary to find such an address.

All these use cases require that the holder of the Bitcoin address in question not only does not mind having his name attached, but actually actively

---

[14] k-lenz.de/bit46.

wants that.

That of course is sacrilege to libertarian purists who require that all Bitcoin transactions should be anonymous.

Well, too bad for them. If I choose to attach my name to a Bitcoin address, who are they to tell me I am not allowed to do that? I am not telling them to attach their names, if they don't want to. And more importantly, what exactly in the Bitcoin protocol stops people from registering their addresses and making such registration public, just as one would make a PGP key public?

As far as I know (I am far from an expert on the technical details of the protocol), the answer to that question is: Nothing.

Like many others I think that there are only two possibilities for the future of the Bitcoin protocol. Either it fails completely, reducing the value of all bitcoin units on the network to zero. Or it becomes mainstream, which would imply a value of individual bitcoins at least 100 times higher than in March 2014, the time of this writing.

And there are not many existential risks that could lead to the first outcome (Bitcoin failing completely). Someone could find an attack against the underlying cryptography. That has not happened for the last couple of years. And it is probably difficult to pull off. But that does not mean it is impossible. If that happens, then it's back to the drawing board for cryptocurrencies, though it may be possible to adopt the protocol so as to make it resilient to such an attack for the future.

More likely is the risk that governments world wide decide that they want to completely ban Bitcoin.

Some of the anarchist libertarian Bitcoin supporters think that would not matter. They think that governments lack the ability to regulate the Bitcoin network even if they tried to.

My answer to that position is that the only way to find out is to see governments try. I don't want to see that.

If governments world wide wanted to shut the Bitcoin network down, here is what their policy would be. Make it illegal to run a bitcoin exchange (easily enforced). Make it illegal to take bitcoins as payment in any business (easily enforced). Make it illegal to publish any research or opinion about the Bitcoin network anywhere (easily enforced in many circumstances). Make it illegal to run a Bitcoin node (easily enforced, you can't run nodes completely anonymous, since traffic needs to reach you somehow). Make it illegal to keep or update a copy of the blockchain. Make it illegal to own bitcoins or to transfer them to someone else. Extend these restrictions to all cryptocurrencies, even to Dogecoin.

If that happens, the Bitcoin protocol may be not completely eradicated. But it would, by definition, be a network used only by criminals. It certainly would never get as mainstream as the Internet is now.

So I for one would be cautious about thinking that governments can't regulate Bitcoin. They most certainly can, and many of the things they could do would have a big impact.

Most of this book is about looking at existing law as it relates to the Bitcoin network, with a focus on Japanese law. Obviously I can't write about the new Japanese Bitcoin Basic Act of 2017 right now (again, in March 2014), though I did write a book titled "Zukünftiges Recht" (Future Law)[15] long ago.

But for the end of this section, one more thought about how Bitcoin regulation might look ten years from now. This is something I wrote on my blog last year, and I am going to just repost it here. The title of that post[16] was "Black Bitcoins and White Bitcoins". Here it is:

---

[15] Karl-Friedrich Lenz, Zukünfiges Recht, k.lenz.name/d/v/zukunft.pdf.
[16] k-lenz.de/btc055.

Some of the important differences between Bitcoin and cash are that all transactions are recorded, all transaction records are kept for eternity, and all transaction records can be seen by anyone.

The NSA probably has a copy of the blockchain somewhere.

This makes the Bitcoin network actually much less attractive for money laundering purposes than both cash and bank transfers. From the point of view of the criminal, the above characteristics are highly undesirable.

While it is true that people can use the Bitcoin network anonymously if they know what they're doing, it is also true that many criminals are stupid. The government may have undercover agents infiltrating money laundering networks. One false move can be enough to tie an address to a real person.

Anyway, for the reasons above I think it would be not appropriate to outlaw the Bitcoin network. For those who insist that can't be done anyway, you are wrong. States can outlaw bitcoins mining (they are already outlawing printing traditional money). They can outlaw running an exchange. They can outlaw accepting bitcoins as a payment for a legitimate Internet business. They could even make it a crime holding bitcoins.

If you want the Bitcoin network to succeed, you don't want any of the above to happen in any country.

But it may well happen. People who stand to lose from the Bitcoin network's success may argue that Bitcoin is an evil instrument of money laundering.

The point of this post is to show that even if that discussion starts in some country or other, there are three possible outcomes. Not two.

Obviously, one can leave it at the present state of affairs, where the Bitcoin network is not illegal (though exchanges might need some license or other already under existing law in some jurisdictions).

Obviously, one could imagine a country going all out in a fight against the Bitcoin network and adopt all of the possible measures discussed above.

But there is a third possibility. One could make black bitcoins illegal and leave white bitcoins untouched.

That, of course, would need a definition. I'll provide it right now.

A white bitcoin would be one tied to a real person. For example, I use the address "1KfLenzKgDW...". I display that fact on this blog. I want it to be public knowledge, for various reasons.

Obviously there are other addresses where the holder of the address is known to the public.

So any bitcoins on this address would be "white" under my definition. That's because this address is completely unsuited for use in any money laundering scheme. The three differences between the Bitcoin network and cash I mentioned at the beginning make any transactions involving this address traceable for anybody, including law enforcement.

On the other hand, Bitcoin addresses that are not linked to any real person would be "black" under my definition. They pose some problems with money laundering. People can move funds with them without attaching their real identities. This is not possible with bank accounts, since under the recommendations of the Financial Action Task Force anonymous bank accounts are not allowed.

The third alternative of allowing only "white bitcoins" would be the equivalent of allowing only bank accounts with real names attached. It would be less restrictive than the second alternative mentioned above, which would ban the white coins with the black coins.

If you want the Bitcoin network to succeed,

you should hope that there is a large amount of white bitcoins in usage, and that criminals are only a small percentage of the whole user base.

Just to be clear, using an address without attaching a name can have legitimate reasons of privacy protection. I'm all for privacy protection. But that does not mean you need to keep all payments anonymous. For most payments, no one cares either way.

And anyway, this post is not so much about discussing whether a law against the Bitcoin network restricted only to black bitcoins would be desirable or not. The main point was to show that there are actually three possible outcomes. Not two. Three.

II. Japanese Policy Discussions

The MtGox insolvency has been big news in Japan. As a result, Japanese politicians are starting to discuss Bitcoin regulation.

These discussions are still only beginning. It is too early to report on any results. And they are very much a moving target, which makes them not very suitable to discuss in a book like this one. Reporting on the latest events in that discussion is better suited to blog posts.

That said, here are a couple of recent developments.

1. First Set of Questions from Opposition

Member of Parliament in the House of Councillors (sangiin, 参議院) Tsutomu Okubo has repeatedly asked the government about Bitcoin. His first set of questions[17] was released on February 25, 2014. I will translate these questions here in full.

The government answered[18] these questions on March 7. I will provide a full translation of these answers as well. Obviously it makes sense to arrange each answer after each question.

Here we go.

(Okubo) "The virtual Internet currency Bitcoin is getting some attention. There are many sites on the Internet that accept bitcoins for the payment of goods or services. An increasing number of brick and mortar merchants are also accepting bitcoins. However, the legal status of Bitcoin is uncertain, which introduces an element of uncertainty to

---

[17] k-lenz.de/btc056.
[18] k-lenz.de/btc057.

payments.

"Therefore, I have the following questions, with a view to clarifying the regulation applying to Bitcoin, and assuring safety and certainty of trades.

"**Question one**: How many bitcoins are in circulation worldwide now, and what is their value in Japanese yen?"

"**Question two**: I understand that the role of Bitcoin for payments and the legal status of Bitcoin is different in various foreign countries. For example, there have been reports that the use of bitcoins has been regulated in China and Russia.

"Are there foreign countries that have adopted a position on the legal status of Bitcoin, or are expected to adopt such a position in the near future?"

(Government) "**Answer to questions one and two**: We understand that there is no specific institution that issues bitcoins. It also lacks the backing of any government or central bank for its credit. The government still does not grasp the big picture of Bitcoin. We are in the process of gathering information, while aiming for an approach coordinated between Ministries involved.

"It is difficult to state anything with certainty

on the question of how many bitcoins are issued right now and what their economic value is. We also don't know if there are any foreign countries who have adopted a legal position on the status of Bitcoin or are in the process of doing so."

(Comment by me): This shows a surprising level of ignorance. The number of bitcoins issued and the market cap at any given moment is easily checked. At the moment I am writing these lines, coinmarketcap.com shows 12,507,525 bitcoins issued and a market capitalization of $7,947,906,761. It takes a couple of moments with a search engine to find this information. The Japanese government could also have easily found the position of the German regulator BaFin issued in 2011[19], which sees bitcoins as "financial instruments", by taking a look at my 2013 paper on the legal issues of Bitcoin[20] (the first such paper in Japanese).

This ignorance will be rectified shortly. But it means that this first government answer can hardly be regarded as being founded on a correct grasp of the

---

[19] Bundesanstalt für Finanzdienstleistungsaufsicht (BaFin), Merkblatt: Hinweise zu dem Gesetz über die Beaufsichtigung von Zahlungsdiensten (Zahlungsdienteaufsichtsgesetz - ZAG), Stand Dezember 2011, k-lenz.de/bit13 www.bafin.de/SharedDocs/Veroeffentlichungen/DE/Merkblatt/mb_111222_zag.html, 4b).
[20] Lenz, Legal Issues of the New Internet Currency Bitcoin in EU Law and German Law, July 2013, k-lenz.de/bitcoin.

situation, as the government itself points out repeatedly.

(Okubo) "**Question three**: Are bitcoins "currency" in Japan under the Civil Code or are they "currency" or "foreign currency" under the Foreign Exchange and Foreign Trade Act? Are there any other laws beside these two that include bitcoins under the term "currency"?

"Also, how is Bitcoin dealt with in the Banking Act, the Financial Instruments and Exchange Act and other laws relating to finance? What is the legal status of Bitcoin in other laws?

(Government) "In Japan, the term currency is regulated for coins in Article 7 of the Act on Currency Units and Issuing of Coins (Act No. 42 of 1987), which allows for issuing up to twenty times of the face value, and for banknotes in Article 46 Paragraph 2 of the Act on the Bank of Japan, which allows for unlimited issuing. These coins and banknotes are recognized as legal tender. In contrast, bitcoins are not currency.

"Currency under Article 402 Paragraph 1 and 2 of the Civil Code are coins and banknotes which have force as legal tender. Since bitcoins have no force as legal tender, they are not currency under these Paragraphs.

"There is also no other law that would include bitcoins in the definition of currency.

"Also, bitcoins are not currency, and they do not as such certify any rights. Therefore, as far as trade in bitcoins as such is concerned, this is not "banking" under Article 2 Paragraph 2 of the Banking Act (Act No. 59 of 1981) or dealing in financial instruments under Article 2 Paragraph 1 and 2 of the Financial Instruments and Exchange Act (Act No. 25 of 1948).

"We are not aware of any other law that defines the legal status of Bitcoin clearly."

(Comment from me): The German regulator disagrees with the idea that trades in bitcoins are free of any oversight. They say that bitcoins are "financial instruments". And it is true that selling one bitcoin for 65,000 yen in a face-to-face deal in Shibuya is not "banking" under the Banking Act. That does not mean, however, that the MtGox exchange was not in the "banking" business. As will be explained in detail below, they certainly were in the banking business the moment they took deposits in traditional currency. Which triggered the requirement for a bank license under Article 4 of the Act.

(Okubo) "**Question four**: If, as a result of the answer to question three above, there is no law in

Japan that would include bitcoins in the definition of currency, is it forbidden in Japan to use bitcoins as a means of payment? If there is such a prohibition, what law exactly would be the basis for that? If there is no such prohibition, I would like to ask about the following three points (including legal basis):

"1. Are trades based on bitcoins taxed?

"2. Is a bank allowed to broker sales of bitcoins, exchange bitcoins for Japanese yen, or offer accounts denominated in bitcoins, or use bitcoins as a means of money transmission?

"3. Can securities firms or firms offering investment advice set up a fund that has bitcoins as their investment target?"

(Government): "As far as we know, there is no law prohibiting the use of bitcoins as a means of payment.

"As far as question 1 is concerned, it is necessary to decide on taxation by looking at individual cases. It is also not clear what the "trades based on bitcoins" in the question exactly are. Therefore it is difficult to provide a general answer.

"As a general rule, if such a trade fulfills the conditions set in the Income Tax Act (Act No. 33 of 1965), the Corporate Tax Act (Act No. 34 of 1965), or the Consumption Tax Act (Act No. 108 of 1988), then it is taxable.

"On question 2, the business of brokering the sale of bitcoins, of exchanging bitcoins for yen, of offering an account denominated in bitcoin, and of transferring money from one such account holder to another, these are all not listed in the businesses allowed to banks under Article 10 Paragraph 1, all Numbers, or Paragraph 2, all Numbers, or Article 11, all Numbers of the Banking Act.

"On question 3, leaving open the question if bitcoins are a suitable target of investing, Article 35 Paragraph 2 Number 6 of the Financial Instruments and Exchange Act and Article 68 Number 19 of the Cabinet Order based on Number 7 of that Paragraph (Cabinet Order No. 52 of 2007) allow securities firms of the first class and securities firms who perform investment services to engage in brokering securities or derivatives, and as rights different from these are concerned as investment of assets, to engage in managing assets."

(Comment from me): Short answer to question three seems to be yes. Barry Silbert of SecondMarket already has set up a "Bitcoin Investment Trust"[21] in the United States, which has

---

[21] See bitcointrust.co for details.

been open for business since the fall of 2013 and is up by over 390% since inception at the time I am writing these lines. I think it would be a very good idea to set up some kind of fund that allows holders of NISA accounts to invest in bitcoins.

NISA accounts are investment accounts where the investor does not need to pay capital gains tax for any investment of up to one million yen a year. The "N" stands for "Nippon", or Japan. The "ISA" part means "individual savings account". Legislation introducing these accounts came into effect in January 2014. But holders of such accounts are not able to invest in the asset class that beat everything else by a large margin last year.

(Okubo) "**Question five**: If bitcoins are actually used in Japan for payment purposes, it becomes necessary to stop such use for money laundering purposes, and to prosecute quickly any such use. In the view of the government, which laws make sure of that? I would like to enquire especially about the Act on Punishment of Organized Crimes and Control of Crime Proceeds and the Act on Prevention of Transfer of Criminal Proceeds in that regard.

"Also, if as an answer to question three there is no law that includes bitcoins in its definition of currency, especially if it is not included in the definitions of the Civil Code, the Banking Act, and the Act on Foreign Exchange and Foreign Trade, I think this may be a problem with money laundering policies, and would like to hear the opinion of the government on that point."

(Government) "Establishing the facts of a crime is a decision to be taken by law enforcement based on the evidence collected in individual cases. The question of using bitcoins for money laundering purposes will be decided by applying Article 10 Paragraph 1 of the Act on Punishment of Organized Crimes and Control of Crime Proceeds (Act No. 136 of 1999). If such an act of using bitcoins falls under "falsifying or concealing the acquisition or disposal" of "proceeds from crime", then a crime under that Article would be committed. Also, the Act on Prevention of Transfer of Criminal Proceeds (Act No. 22 of 2007) requires specified business operators under Article 2 Paragraph 2 of that act to follow "Know-Your-Customer" rules for certain trades, regardless if bitcoins are used or not.

"As already mentioned in our answer to question 3 above, there is no law that would include bitcoins in its definition of currency. The question if this fact will be a problem for money laundering policies is difficult to answer at this stage, since the real circumstances of bitcoins use are not clear at the moment."

(Okubo) "**Question six**: Exchanges for trading bitcoins against Japanese yen, American dollars or other foreign currencies exist also in Japan. Is the establishment of such an exchange or are the trades conducted there void under the Civil Code? Are these compatible with the Banking Act, the Financial Instruments and Exchange Act, the Act on Foreign Exchange and Foreign Trade, and other laws? I would like to ask especially about the crimes of gambling and selling lottery tickets under the Criminal Code."

(Government) "There is no law generally prohibiting the establishment of exchanges for trading bitcoins against Japanese yen, American dollars or other foreign currencies, or the trades conducted there. The question if these are void under the Civil Code or in violation of other laws needs to be decided on a case by case basis. It is not possible to give a general answer."

(Okubo) "**Question seven**: Offering trading between bitcoins and Japanese yen, American dollars or other foreign currencies may be offering a fake investment or a pyramid scheme. Is there any criminal penalty for that? Also, what kind of registration or compliance with offering regulations under the Financial Instruments and Exchange Act and other laws regulating finance are necessary for opening an exchange?"

(Government) "There is no law that generally provides a criminal sanction for opening a bitcoin exchange. Therefore it is to be decided on a case-by-case basis if such an offering violates criminal law. Also, as explained already in the answer to question three, trades in bitcoins do not qualify as trades in securities etc., so there is no need for registering or compliance with offering regulation for this kind of trade."

(Comment from me): As will be shown in detail below, operating an exchange like MtGox certainly requires a bank license. That has nothing to do with Bitcoin. They were taking deposits in traditional money. That triggers a license requirement under Article 3 of the Banking Act. Therefore, this answer seems to be lacking somewhat. If bitcoin exchanges are completely unregulated, that's a recipe for the next disaster like the MtGox mess to happen.

2. Second Set of Questions from Opposition

Okubo followed up with another set of

questions[22] the following week. Again, I am going to provide a full translation of these questions (and their answer by the government) below.

Here we go.

(Okubo) "Since I had some doubts about the government's answers to my last set of questions about Bitcoin, I add the questions below:

"**Question one**: In answer to my question, the Bank of Japan delivered a report. According to that report, there are about 12 million bitcoins issued. At the rate of February 27 of this year (one bitcoin was at $621), that would be the equivalent of about $7.7 billion. Looking at these numbers, one can say that bitcoins are on their way to being recognized as a method of payment and investment.

"Considering these facts, what is the government's position on the opinion that bitcoin provides its users with a method of measuring value, storing value, and exchanging value?"

(Government) "The government does not yet understand the big picture regarding Bitcoin. We are in the process of gathering information,

---

[22] k-lenz.de/btc062.

coordinating the efforts of relevant Ministries. There are many different statements about the amount of bitcoins issued, and their price. Therefore, as we answered the last time, it is difficult to make a definite statement about the amount of bitcoins issued and their market capitalization. Therefore, it is difficult to state a position about the opinion mentioned in the question."

(Comment by me): It is hard to believe that the government would not know such basic facts. If they still have not been able to figure this out, the "coordinated effort to gather information" does not seem to be progressing very well.

Even if you don't know how many bitcoins there are, you could still discuss the question of whether the Bitcoin network functions as money that was raised in the question.

(Okubo) "**Question two**: In the answer to my previous questions one and two the government states: 'We are in the process of gathering information, while aiming for an approach coordinated between the Ministries involved.' But, considering the bitcoin market capitalization of $7.7, the petition for civil rehabilitation filed by the MtGox stock company, and other recent developments, I think that it would be desirable to speed up the information gathering and provide the necessary regulation quickly.

"When does the government intend to legislate in this area? Especially, I would like to ask for clarification if it is possible to get this done in the current legislative period."

(Government) "With regard to Bitcoin, the government is now in the process of gathering information in an effort coordinated between relevant Ministries. Once we understand the big picture, we will proceed to thinking about necessary policies. Therefore, we can not give any certain answer on the question if we plan to legislate, and if so, when that will happen."

(Comment by me): The bright side is that the government has not committed to any position right now. That means interested parties can still contribute to the discussion. Having no position is much better than a knee-jerk reaction with legislation not thought through.

(Okubo) "**Question three**: In the answer to my previous question three, the terms "legal tender" and "force as legal tender" are used.

"1. How does the government understand the terms "legal tender" and "force as legal tender"? If these terms are based on laws, what are these laws, and where are the definitions for these terms?

"2. Which is the subject that assures "legal

tender" or "force as legal tender"? Especially, I would like this point explained for foreign currency traded in Japan.

"3. In Japan, American dollars, renminbi, Indian rupees and other foreign currencies are not recognized with force as legal tender. Considering that, one may think that bitcoins have the same quality as these foreign currencies. What does the government think about this point? If the government disagrees, please state the reasons for that."

(Government) "1. The term "force as legal tender" as used in our last answer means that if the debtor of a claim of money uses the medium in question to fulfill his obligation, the creditor cannot refuse this as performance, and the performance becomes valid as a matter of course. For coins this force as legal tender is ordered by Article 7 of the Act on Currency Units and Issuing of Coins (Act No. 42 of 1987), which allows for issuing up to twenty times the face value, and for banknotes in Article 46 Paragraph 2 of the Act on the Bank of Japan, which allows for unlimited issuing.

"2. The "force as legal tender" is guaranteed by the sovereign State, or by an equivalent entity. Foreign currency is currency for which a foreign country recognizes force as legal tender. Foreign currency does not have force as legal tender in Japan.

"3. As stated above, foreign currency has force of legal tender in a foreign country. Since there is no state recognizing bitcoins as legal tender, it is difficult to understand bitcoins as an equivalent to foreign currency."

(Comment by me): This answer shows that the government is right when asserting they don't understand Bitcoin yet. I will discuss this question in detail below. But, in short, when talking about the situation in Japan, both bitcoins and American dollars lack force as legal tender. And the freedom of contracts allows parties to recognize the force as legal tender for a specific contract both for dollars and bitcoins.

(Okubo) "**Question four**: In the answer to my previous question 4-2, the government states that brokering the sale of bitcoins, offering an account denominated in bitcoins, or providing payment services with bitcoins are not businesses allowed to banks.

"Can banks buy bitcoins for themselves? Can they set up an investment trust? Can they set up derivative investment schemes based on bitcoins? Please explain if these business activities are allowed under the law, and the Articles this is based on, or the conditions that apply."

(Government) "The act of buying bitcoins in the question is not a business listed as a bank business activity in Article 10 Paragraph 1 all numbers, Paragraph 2 all numbers, or Article 11 all numbers.

"It is correct that a bank can engage in the business activity of buying and selling securities (Article 10 Paragraph 2 Number 2), the business activity of trading in security and financial derivatives (Paragraph 2 Numbers 2, 12, and 14). However, since it is not entirely clear what is meant by "bitcoin investment trusts" or "investment schemes based on bitcoins" in the question, it is difficult to give a general answer.

"On the other hand, as long as "buying bitcoins" does not reach the level of a business activity, while it may be open to debate if that would be appropriate, this would be dealt with like a bank buying other assets not directly related to their business activities. There is no provision in the Banking Act that would clearly prohibit such an act.

(Okubo) "**Question five**: Is the business of offering put options on bitcoins, for example the derivative right to buy one bitcoin at $500, a business listed in the relevant laws for institutions taking deposits, enabling these institutions to offer such derivaties? For example, with banks that would be the Articles 10 and 11 of the Banking Act, and for securities brokers it would be Article 35 of the Financial Instruments and Exchange Act. If this is possible, I would also like to ask if these are legally classified as specific business or incidental business.

Another business would be offering a saving plan or a financial instrument the value of which changes with the price of bitcoins. I would like to know if financial deposit institutions or securities brokers can set up, issue, or broker such investments."

(Government) "Under Article 10 Paragraph 2 Number 2, Number 12, and Number 14 of the Banking Act, a bank may engage as a business activity intrinsic to banking in trading in securities or financial derivatives. Under Article 35 Paragraph 4 of the Financial Instruments and Exchange Act a securities broker may engage in business activities, beside those of brokering and those regulated in Paragraph 1 and 2 of that Article, for which they have received a special permit from the Prime Minister. However, since it is not clear what exactly the meaning of an "option on bitcoins, for example the derivative right to buy one bitcoin at $500" is supposed to mean, it is difficult to give a general answer if this would fall under these rules.

"Also, Article 13-4 of the Banking Act allows banks to accept deposits set up in a way that they are linked to market indexes or other indexes. Article 2 Paragraph 8 Number 1 and 2 of the Financial Instruments and Exchange Act allow securities brokers to engage in the business of selling and buying financial instruments, brokering such sales, and acting as intermediary for them. However, since it is not clear what exactly "offering a saving plan or financial instrument the value of which changes with the price of bitcoins" is supposed to mean, it is difficult to give a general answer if this would fall under these rules."

(Okubo) "**Question six**: Since the government thinks that bitcoins are no currency, I would like to know the government's position on if it is not illegal for someone to take deposits of bitcoins from a multitude of unspecified customers, guaranteeing the capital, or to lend those bitcoins in a continuing basis, under the Act Regulating the Receipt of Contributions, the Receipt of Deposits, and Interest Rates[23]. If the government thinks taking such deposits is illegal, I would like to know the detailed interpretation such an opinion is based on.

"Also, if someone lends 100 bitcoins at an interest of 30 bitcoins a year, receiving 130 bitcoins

---

[23] Law No. 195 of June 23, 1954, k-lenz.de/btc007.

back, would in the government's opinion such a contract using bitcoins be possible even if the interest is above the interest rates allowed by the Interest Rate Restriction Act[24] and the Act Regulating the Receipt of Contributions, the Receipt of Deposits, and Interest Rates?"

(Government) "It is not clear what exactly "to take deposits of bitcoins from a multitude of unspecified customers, guaranteeing the capital, or to lend these bitcoins on a continuing basis" is supposed to mean. Also, establishing the facts of a crime is a decision to be taken by law enforcement based on the evidence collected in individual cases. Therefore, we can only make some general statements. As far as the Act of Regulating the Receipt of Contributions, the Receipt of Deposits, and Interest Rates (Act No. 95 of 1954) is concerned, if the criminal sanctions rules in that Act are violated, it would be illegal under that Act. As to the question which laws might be violated in that case, that would be a matter decided by looking at the circumstances of the concrete case at hand. Furthermore, regarding the question of the application of Article 1 of the Interest Rate Restriction Act (Act No. 100 of 1954): This rule makes void contracts about lending money as far as the interest rate stated in each Number of that Article

---

[24] Act No. 100 of 15 May 1954, k-lenz.de/btc063.

is surpassed. The question if this rule would be applicable to the lending of bitcoins is difficult to answer, since it is not clear how bitcoins are used."

(Okubo) "**Question seven**: The MtGox stock company was the World's largest exchange before it filed a petition for opening a civil rehabilitation procedure. On the other hand, there is a report by the American Congressional Research Service[25] which states that bitcoins may be used for money laundering purposes. There is also a case in which one of the board members of an institution promoting Bitcoin was arrested. (Note by me: This refers to the arrest of former Bitcoin Foundation board member Charlie Shrem[26]).

"Under these circumstances one could think that financial institutions offering accounts to MtGox and other bitcoin exchanges in Japan would have a obligation to enhanced due diligence. What does the government think of such an opinion? If there is such an obligation, I would also like to know the extent of such an obligation.

---

[25] Congressional Research Service, Bitcoin: Questions, Answers, and Legal Issues, Craig K. Elwell, M. Maureen Murphy, Michael V. Seitzinger, December 20, 2013, www.fas.org/sgp/crs/misc/R43339.pdf.
[26] Kyle Russel, Meet the 'Bitcoin Millionaire' Arrested for Allegedly Help Silk Road Luander $1 Million, Business Insider, k-lenz.de/btc065.

"Also, if someone wires large sums of money into the account of a bitcoin exchange that is offered by a bank for the purpose of buying bitcoins, has the bank in question a duty to make sure of the identity of the person wiring the money, confirm if there are bitcoins bought with that money or not, and hold on to documents about the identity of the person wiring the money? I would also like to know if the government has plans to introduce any such enhanced due diligence obligations."

(Government) "It is not clear what exactly "enhanced due diligence regarding money laundering" is supposed to mean. For example, Article 8 Paragraph 1 of the Act on Prevention of Transfer of Criminal Proceeds (Act No. 22 of 2007) (Criminal Proceeds Act) requires financial institutions that accept deposits or savings to report to the authorities specified in Article 21 of the Crime Proceeds Act in certain cases. If assets they receive in their business are suspected of being proceeds of a crime, or if the customer is suspected of having violated the Act on Organized Crimes and Control of Crime Proceeds (Act No. 94 of 1991), then they need to report. It does not matter in that case if the customer in question is a "bitcoin exchange" or not.

"Also, under the Crime Proceeds Act, if there is a wire transfer to some account, financial institutions are under no obligation to confirm the identity of the person wiring the money, or the purpose of the wire transfer, or to hold on to records of the transaction. It does not matter for that if the account in question is that of a "bitcoin exchange" or not. Also, a bank that receives a request for a wire transfer needs to confirm the identity of the person wiring the money, the purpose of the wire transfer, and needs to hold on to records of the transaction, if the wire transfer is done by deposition more than 100,000 yen, or in other cases prescribed by the Criminal Proceeds Act."

(Okubo) "Question eight: If someone runs a bitcoin exchange in Japan, are they obliged to register in some way, or report in some way, in the opinion of the government? I would also like to know the relevant law regulating bitcoin exchanges, and the Ministry in charge."

(Government) "It is not exactly clear what business model the "bitcoin exchange" in the question is supposed to take. But as far as the business activity of exchanging bitcoins and currency, there is no rule in Japanese law that would require such an exchange to register or report to the relevant Ministry, and there is no "Ministry in charge".

(Okubo) "**Question nine**: If someone runs a bitcoin exchange in Japan, do they have any obligations regarding anti-money laundering measures, like recording facts, or reporting the value of bitcoin trades or withdrawals to the relevant Ministry, in the opinion of the government?"

(Government) "As we said in our last answer to question three, there is no law in Japan that clearly regulates Bitcoin. Also, since the concrete circumstances of the "bitcoin exchange" in the question are not exactly clear, it is difficult to give a general answer.

(Okubo) "**Question ten**: In the answer to my last question three the government says that bitcoins are not currency or a foreign currency. Does the government think bitcoins are tangible things like gold or antiques, or does it think they are electronic records?

"Also, if the government thinks bitcoins are electromagnetic records, is an act of illegal access to a computer and changing the records on bitcoins an act of computer fraud?"

(Government) "It is not clear what exactly "tangible things" in the question are supposed to mean. Anyway, since the use of Bitcoin is not clear at the moment, it is difficult to answer if bitcoins are "tangible things" or electromagnetic records.

"Establishing the facts of a crime is a decision to be taken by law enforcement based on the evidence collected in individual cases. However, as a general rule, if a person obtains or causes another to obtain a profit by creating a false electromagnetic record relating to acquisition, loss or alteration of property rights by inputting false data or giving unauthorized commands to a computer utilized for the business of another, or by putting a false electromagnetic record relating to acquisition, loss, or alteration of property rights into use for the administration of the matters of another, then such an act would qualify as computer fraud."

(Okubo) "**Question eleven**: If a Japanese company exports luxury goods like watches, perfume, or caviar via a third country to North Korea, receives payment in bitcoins and exchanges these bitcoins on an exchange into yen, is such a business without problems under existing laws? If there is a problem, what statutes would apply and which Ministry would be responsible?

"Also, if someone living in Japan transfers one hundred million yen worth of bitcoins to someone in North Korea, is such an act without problems under existing laws? If there is some kind of reporting obligation, or an obligation to receive a permit, I would like to know the reason and the applicable law."

(Government) According to Article 10 and 48, Paragraph 3 of the Foreign Trade and Foreign Exchange Act (Act No. 228 of 1949) (below "Foreign Exchange Act"), if the final destination of freight is North Korea, it is necessary for such export to obtain the permission of the Economy Minister, even if the trade is done via a third country. Since such a permission will not be given except for humanitarian reasons, export of luxury goods is in violation of the Foreign Exchange Act. The fact of payment in bitcoins does not change that either way.

"As for the question if somebody transfers bitcoins worth 100,000,000 yen from Japan to North Korea, that would require a report under Article 55 of the Foreign Exchange Act if that was a "payment" under that Article.

"However, if that payment was done for an import that has either North Korea as country of origin or was loaded into a ship in North Korea, and that import has not received a permit under Article 52 of the Foreign Exchange Act, it is prohibited under Article 16 Paragraph 5 of the Foreign Exchange Act, and in violation of that Act.

"Also, if that payment is to a person specified

as connected with the North Korean missile or weapons of mass destruction program, or if it is done with the purpose of contributing to North Korea's nuclear weapons, missiles, or other weapons of mass destruction programs, such a payment needs permission by the Ministry in charge under Article 60 of the Foreign Exchange Act."

(Okubo) "Question twelve: In answer to my last question four, the government said that as a general principle, Bitcoin could be an object of taxation under the Income Tax Act and the Corporate Tax Act.

"1. If someone who has gained an economic advantage from trading in bitcoins declares his income, what is the correct category of such income, as a general rule? Is it capital gains? I would also like to receive an explanation on how to deal with these issues as a matter of corporate tax."

(Government) "It is necessary to decide case by case on individual taxation issues. Also, it is not exactly clear what "gained an economic advantage from trading in bitcoins" means. Therefore it is difficult to give a general answer. As a general rule, economic advantages gained by an individual are capital gains if they meet the conditions of Article 33 of the Income Tax Act (Act No. 33 of 1965). For economic advantages gained by a legal person, that economic advantage would be included in the calculation of income of that legal person for the business year involved."

"2. If someone not living in Japan or a foreign corporation gained such an advantage from trading on an exchange in Japan, is it correct to assume that as a general rule such gains would be taxable, in the opinion of the government?"

(Government) "It is necessary to decide case by case on individual taxation issues. Also, it is not exactly clear what "gained an economic advantage from trading in bitcoins at an exchange based in Japan" means. Therefore it is difficult to give a general answer. As a general rule, non-residents of Japan under Article 2 Paragraph 1 Number 5 or foreign legal persons under Article 2 Number 4 of the Corporate Tax Act (Act No. 34 of 1965) are taxable in Japan for income in Japan, as defined under Article 7 Paragraph 1 Number 3 and Number 5 of the Income Tax Act and Article 9 Paragraph 1 of the Corporate Tax Act. If some income does not qualify as "income in Japan" under these Articles, it is not subject to Japanese taxation."

(Okubo) "**Question thirteen**: If someone has gained an economic advantage from trading in bitcoins, would he need to report in his form declaring the amount of assets and obligations? Also, is that something he would need to report under the system on reporting assets outside of Japan, in the opinion of the government? If bitcoins need to be included in these reports, I would also like to know under which category bitcoins fall, in the opinion of the government.

(Government) "It is not clear what "economic advantage gained from trading in bitcoins" is supposed to mean. Therefore it is difficult to give a general answer. As a general rule, the form declaring assets required by Article 232 Paragraph 1 of the Income Tax Act needs to be filled out according to the rules specified in Table 10 of the Ordinance on the Income Tax Act (Finance Ministry Ordinance 11 of 1965). And the report required under Article 5 Paragraph 1 of the Act on Submission of Overseas Wire Transfers for Purpose of Securing Proper Domestic Taxation (Act No. 110 of 1997) is to be filed according to the rules specified in the Ordinance on the Act on Submission of Overseas Wire Transfers for Purpose of Securing Proper Domestic Taxation (Finance Ministry Ordinance No 96 of 1997)."

(Okubo) "Question fourteen: In the answer to my last question four, the government said that bitcoin transaction may as a general rule be subject to consumption tax. If for example on a bitcoin exchange in Japan one bitcoin was sold for fifty thousand yen, does that mean that at present tax rates there would be a consumption tax of 2,500 yen to be paid, in the opinion of the government? In that case, does the consumption tax also apply to the fees of the exchange, and the fees for wiring the money? Also, if there is a consumption tax obligation, who would be the person obliged to pay that tax?"

(Government) "It is necessary to decide case by case on individual taxation issues. Also, it is not exactly clear what "one bitcoin was sold for fifty thousand yen at an exchange based in Japan" means. Therefore it is difficult to give a general answer. As a general rule, if this is disposing of an asset under Article 4 Paragraph 1 of the Consumption Tax Act (Act No. 108 of 1988), and it does not fall under one of the exceptions under Article 6 Paragraph 1 of that Act, it would be subject to consumption tax.

"Also, as to the person obliged to pay the tax, it is the business that has disposed of the asset, except if it is one exempt under Article 9 Paragraph 1 of that Act."

III. Currency?

As explained in the preceding section, the Japanese government does not see bitcoins as a currency in March 2014.

I disagree with that point of view. The Bitcoin network was designed as a payment system, and bitcoins are currency units allowed on that payment system. Of course bitcoins are a currency. Not only are they a currency, they are the strongest currency of the World, backed by the most trustworthy institution on the planet, the blockchain.

The Japanese government is correct in part. Indeed, bitcoins do not have the force of legal tender. They can be used as a method of payment only if the creditor voluntary agrees with that use. In contrast, Article 402 of the Civil Code [27] says that money obligations in Japan are to be paid in Japanese yen, which do have the force of legal tender.

But that does not mean that a creditor can't accept bitcoins instead. And under the general principle of freedom of contracts, the parties of a contract are free to agree on bitcoins as a payment method in the first place, in which case the obligation to pay will be denominated in bitcoins, and not in Japanese yen. And that obligation has legal force. As long as there is no prohibition against using bitcoins in Japan (there is none right now), such a contract is valid. The principle of freedom of contracts means

---

[27] k-lenz.de/btc059.

that, yes, an obligation to pay some amount or other of bitcoins created by a contract is enforcable, just like an obligation to pay in Japanese yen, or Mongolian tögrögs, or American dollars.

It is none of the business of the government which of these alternatives the parties of a private contract prefer.

This is the legal argument. Now for a couple of remarks on the economic side.

The price of bitcoins has gone up against the Japanese yen by an average factor of ten for the last couple of years. There is no other currency in the World that has performed so well. It takes over 60,000 Japanese yen to buy one single bitcoin at the time of this writing. There is no other currency where one single unit is valued so high. This makes bitcoins not only some currency, but the strongest currency in the World.

And, in my opinion, bitcoins are backed by the most trustworthy institution of the world, the blockchain.

In contrast to Japanese yen, it is utterly impossible to forge even one bitcoin. Japanese banknotes can be forged. There is a provision in the

Criminal Code[28] that makes such forgery a crime, in Article 148. There is no such provision for bitcoins, and there is no need for it, since it is impossible for anyone to forge a bitcoin in the first place. There is no provision in the Criminal Code for making the Moon drop down on the Earth either, and it is not needed for exactly the same reason.

Also, in contrast to Japanese yen, it is impossible to increase the amount of bitcoins in circulation without changing the Bitcoin protocol, which can only be done with the consent of a majority of miners. That is one of the core features that make bitcoins a much stronger currency than any of the traditional currencies. There is no way to devalue everyone's money by printing more.

So, to sum up the previous couple of paragraphs, bitcoins are impossible to forge, their supply is completely fixed, and as a result their value has been skyrocketing. Therefore, bitcoins have been an excellent choice in the last couple of years for the purpose of storing value, which is one of the functions a currency needs to perform.

And those higher prices are not just some sort of bubble. They are based on the fact that the Bitcoin network is growing exponentially every single day.

---

[28] k-lenz.de/btc027.

The number of users, the raw calculating power of the computers that mine the blockchain, the number of merchants accepting bitcoins as payments, and other similar indicators can be used to measure that growth, and compare it with other cryptocurrencies like Litecoin or Dogecoin. There is an objective reason that bitcoins are valued higher than litecoins, and it lies in the greater power of the Bitcoin network compared to the Litecoin network. The higher prices are not just a bubble. They reflect the power and the exponential growth of the Bitcoin network.

That of course means that as the Bitcoin network growth continues, the price of bitcoins will go up even more. Eventually the Bitcoin network will be as mainstream as the Internet itself. Once that happens, I for one expect that the value of one bitcoin will grow by at least another factor of one hundred from present levels. It is $638 as I write these lines, just for later reference.

The other function a currency needs to perform is a means of payment. The Bitcoin network is superior to all existing payment systems.

It is superior to bank wire transfers, since it is both faster and cheaper. There is the added advantage that users can, if they choose to do so, handle these transfers themselves. The basic idea of the Bitcoin network is to add payment functionality to the peer-to-peer Internet. Just as you don't need a publisher anymore to publish a book, you don't need a bank anymore to pay someone.

It is superior to credit cards, since it is faster, cheaper, and safer. The first aspect needs a bit of discussion. With the Bitcoin network, confirmations take around ten minutes. One might object that this makes payments slower than with a credit card. But actually the opposite is true. An unconfirmed Bitcoin transaction is valid immediately. There only remains the possibility of a double spend in the ten minute time window. In contrast, with a credit card, the card holder can reverse the payment by disputing the transactions for months. The transaction does not become final in ten minutes, but only after the deadline for disputing the credit card payment has passed.

Payments over the Bitcoin network can be done without any fee, or with a small miner's fee. They are cheaper than credit card fees. That advantage is significant if you are a merchant and like the idea of reducing your costs.

And payments with credit cards are unsafe on principle. Everyone who gets paid with a credit card receives all information necessary to abuse that credit card. They can go ahead and use that credit card for fraud themselves. Or some thieves may hack their servers and steal the customers' credit card information. All of those headaches disappear with the Bitcoin network. You don't give your private keys to anyone when paying with bitcoins.

Payment with bitcoins is also superior to paying with cash. If you take cash in your brick and mortar business, you need to count the cash at the end of the day. And then you need to transport it safely to your bank.

With the Bitcoin network, the counting is done automatically. And there is no need to transport anything from the point of sale to some bank or other. The people working at the store do not need to know any private keys. One can set up the whole payment flow in a way that stores any private keys only at some remote server. That of course means that there is no more incentive for someone to try to rob a cash register. There is no cash accessible for people working at the store, which means there is none accessible to robbers either.

Some people may dispute these advantages. But it is impossible to dispute that the Bitcoin network actually works as a means of settling payments, exactly what it was devised for. People are doing more and more business with bitcoin payments.

Bitpay alone reached $100 million [29] in processed payments already in December of 2013.

So to sum up these short observations on economic factors, yes, bitcoins are an excellent store of value, the best currency there is on the planet for that purpose. And, yes, bitcoins are an excellent payment method, superior to everything existing before.

IV. Copyright Protection?

At this point of the development of Bitcoin law, there is still much confusion. As noted above, I think that bitcoins are a currency. The network was designed as a currency, is used as a currency, and succeeds as a currency.

But some, like the Japanese government, do not share that view.

If one thinks that bitcoins are not a currency, it is somewhat difficult to find an adequate way of treating them under the law. One possible idea is a suggestion made by Masaichi Tsuchiya in a recent

---

[29] Emily Spaven, Merchants Love Bitcoin, and Bitpay has 100 Million Reasons to Prove It, December 11, 2013 (Coindesk), k-lenz.de/btc092.

paper[30] on the treatment of Bitcoin under Japanese tax law. The author floats the idea of protecting bitcoins under copyright law.

I'll provide a short translation of the idea as developed on page eight of that paper. Then I will discuss it.

"Is there copyright protection for individual bitcoins? Individual bitcoins are only a pattern of bits. But as explained above, for mining bitcoins it is necessary to expend a vast effort in trying out alternatives. Therefore, they can be viewed as the result of an intellectual process. Therefore they are a creative expression of thoughts belonging to the field of science, and therefore may be viewed as protected works under copyright law. Under Japanese copyright law it is possible to transfer the copyright under a work completely to another person. However, copyright for works published anonymously expires fifty years after publication. That means that from 2060 on some bitcoins will drop out of copyright protection. Anyway, the question if bitcoins are works under copyright law needs to be discussed by copyright specialists."

I have some interest in copyright. So I

---

[30] Masaichi Tsuchiya, Bittokoin to zeimu (Bitcoin and tax practice), Zeidai Journal 2014, 4, k-lenz.de/btc101.

welcome the opportunity to discuss this proposal.

One problem is that for copyright protection you need a human author. Mining bitcoins is not a process where one or more human authors express some thought or other. Miners pay for hardware and electricity. Then they lean back and wait for their hardware to solve a block. Their thoughts are not expressed in any way if they successfully find such a block.

It is true, as Tsuchiya points out in his article, that solving a block involves a vast amount of computing work. However, copyright protection is not granted because someone invested a lot of effort. It protects creative expression, not investment in hardware.

Therefore I don't think there is much merit to the idea in general. There is however one special case that might be seen somewhat differently.

That is the case of a brain wallet[31] based on a work protected by copyright.

A "brain wallet" is created by taking any input and applying a SHA256 hash to it. The input can be a work protected by copyright. Any work.

---

[31] Bitcoin Wiki, Article "Brain Wallet", k-lenz.de/btc102.

Obviously it is not a good idea to take only one work and use it without any changes. But adding some information or using several works in combination may be secure enough for many situations.

In that case, the work the bitcoin address is based on clearly is protected by copyright. Does that protection extend to the resulting bitcoin address? Would that be a derivative work under copyright?

I don't think so, and for the same reasons bitcoins are not protected under copyright in the first place.

Whatever calculations are performed for transforming the input into a bitcoin address are done mechanically by a computer. There is no creative expression by a human author involved. The result will be meaningless to any human reader. And it will be impossible to reverse the process (restore the original work from the bitcoin address).

In conclusion, this is an interesting idea. But I don't think it is possible to extend copyright protection to individual bitcoins.

CHAPTER 2:
LICENSING AND OVERSIGHT

I. Banking License

1. Statutes

When you are dealing with law, there are primary sources and secondary sources. Primary sources are statutes and court decisions. Secondary sources are books (like this one) or articles discussing, translating, or explaining these primary sources.

a) Banking Act

In Japanese law, the main primary source is the statute. In this case, the Japanese Banking Act. Since I am writing in the English language here, the first order of business is to find a translation for that statute.

Fortunately, such a translation is available on the government-sponsored website "Japanese Law Translation"[32]. Banking Act, Law Number 59 of 1981.

The relevant Articles are, in order:

---

[32] k-lenz.de/btc006.

Article 1 Paragraph 1, which sets down the purposes of the Banking Act. It reads like this:

"(1) The purpose of this Act is, in view of the public nature of banking services and for the purpose of maintaining their credibility, securing protection for depositors, etc. and facilitating the smooth functioning of financial services, to ensure the sound and appropriate operations of banking services, thereby contributing to the sound development of the national economy."

The important part here is "protection for depositors". As Koyama explains [33], it is of vital importance that the general public can safely deposit their funds and be assured that they will be paid back with interest. To achieve that purpose, it is necessary to regulate any business taking deposits.

The definition of the term "Banking", which is the activity restricted to banks with a license, is found in Article 2, Paragraph 2 of the law, which reads like this:

"(2) The term "Banking" as used in this Act means commercial pursuits carried out through any of the following acts:

---

[33] Koyama, Yoshiaki, Shoukai ginkouhou (Detailed explanation of the Banking Act), second edition 2012, 56.

(i) Acceptance of deposits or Installment Savings, in addition to loans of fund, or the discounting of bills and notes; or

(ii) Carrying out of exchange transactions."

This definition is supplemented by Article 3, which extends the scope of the "Banking" term. It reads:

"Any commercial pursuit involving acceptance of deposits or Installment Savings etc. (excluding those falling under acts listed in paragraph (2) item (i) of the preceding Article) shall be deemed to be Banking and this Act shall apply."

There are other relevant Articles. I won't quote them in full, however. They are only common sense. Article 4 requires a license for "Banking" activities. Article 61 supplements this with a criminal law provision. If someone is "Banking" without a license, they get a fine of up to three million yen, a prison sentence of up to three years, or both.

b) Receipt of Deposits Act

There is also a similar statute in the Act Regulating the Receipt of Contributions, the Receipt of Deposits, and Interest Rates[34]. Since that title is very long, I will refer to this Act as the "Receipt of Deposits Act".

Article 2 of that Law states:

"(Prohibition on the Receipt of Deposits)

(1) A person other than one whose receipt of deposits in the course of trade is specially provided for in other Acts may not receive deposits in the course of trade.

(2) The terms "receive deposits" and "receipt of deposits" as set forth in the preceding paragraph means the receipt of monies from numerous, unspecified persons, as prescribed in the following items:

(i) the receipt of deposits, savings, or installment savings;

(ii) company bonds, borrowings or any other thing under any other name with the same economic nature as what is prescribed in the preceding item."

There was a similar restriction against taking deposits before this law was enacted, but it was applicable only to lending businesses. Since at the time there was a wave of depositors losing money

---

[34] Law No. 195 of June 23, 1954, k-lenz.de/btc007.

deposited at shady lending businesses, the range of the statute was extended to everyone[35]. Just like the Banking Act does not require loaning of funds for the restriction on taking deposits without a license to apply (Article 3), the Receipt of Deposits Act in its present form is applicable to everyone. It doesn't matter for what purpose the deposits in question are supposed to be used.

There is a criminal law provision in that Act as well, and just like the Banking Act, running an operation receiving deposits without a license is punishable by up to three years in prison or a fine of up to three million yen (Article 8 Paragraph 3).

That is worth quoting in full as well, since it has a provision against circumventing the statute:

"(3) A person who falls under either of the following items is subject to imprisonment with work for not more than three years, a fine of not more than 3,000,000 yen, or both:

(i) a person who violates the provisions of Article 1, Article 2 (1), Article 3, or Article 4 (1) or (2);

(ii) a person who evades the prohibitions set forth in the preceding item, regardless of the name in

---

[35] Nobuhide Majima, Shusshihou daini jou ni okeru azukarikin no kinshi, Ajia Hougaku 43-2, 75, 76-77 (2009).

which or the means by which the person has done so."

Since the Receipt of Deposits Act has this prohibition of evasion of the legal obligations, it is broader than the equivalent Article 61 of the Banking Law.

It may also be of interest to note that the Receipt of Deposits Act does not require a profit motive. As Koyama explains[36], the wording is wider than Article 3 of the Banking Act.

2. Relation to the MtGox Business Model

With the text of the relevant statutes clear now, let's take a look at how they relate to the MtGox business model.

The business model of the MtGox exchange is to take deposits in actual money or in bitcoins from customers.

It is possible to run a bitcoin exchange in a different way. The German exchange bitcoin.de is operating in that different way. They don't take deposits of actual money.

---

[36] Koyama, Yoshiaki, Shoukai ginkouhou (Detailed explanation of the Banking Act), second edition 2012, 66-68.

Customers at bitcoin.de are contracting directly. The exchange does not act as a central counterparty.

If you want to buy bitcoins there, you need to register. But you don't ever deposit actual money at the exchange. A buyer uses the system to find a seller that offers conditions the buyer agrees with. If he finds a seller, he can accept the sales offer over the exchange platform.

Then he proceeds to pay the seller directly. Payment must be done within 60 minutes of the sale, over online banking.

The seller then confirms that he received the payment. Again, for the purpose here the only point relevant is that the actual money never touches the exchange. That means that as far as a banking license for depositing actual money is concerned, with this business model that would be not necessary.

The recent bitcoin exchange opened by SecondMarket[37] in the United States has a similar business model. According to an article by Pete Rizzo at Coindesk[38] the way to buy bitcoins on that exchange is like this:

---

[37] Transact in Bitcoin with SecondMarket, k-lenz.de/btc009.
[38] Pete Rizzo, SecondMarket Takes a First Step to Becoming a US Bitcoin Exchange, February 7, 2014, k-lenz.de/btc008.

Both sellers and buyers need to register with SecondMarket and fill out a "New Account Profile" form. SecondMarket is a registered broker-dealer regulated by the SEC and FINRA and is therefore required to comply with anti-money laundering and know your customer regulations. Once the new account profile form is filed, customers are required to pass further "compliance steps".

Then, sellers and buyers discuss the price and the number of bitcoins offline. Once both sides are happy with the result, the seller sends the bitcoins to SecondMarket. The buyer pays the funds directly to the seller (as with the German exchange discussed above). Then, once the seller confirms payment, SecondMarket releases the bitcoins to the buyer.

In this model, the exchange doesn't touch any actual money at any time. But they do accept a deposit of bitcoins, though only for the brief time needed to finish the transaction.

If one wanted to get rid of that bitcoin depositing step, it would actually be very easy. The Bitcoin protocol has escrow transactions built in[39]. The seller can send the bitcoins directly to the buyer's Bitcoin address with a transaction that requires SecondMarket to sign for having the bitcoins go

---

[39] See the explanation at the Bitcoin Wiki k-lenz.de/btc010.

either to the buyer or back to the seller.

Back to the MtGox business model. In contrast to the German bitcoin.de platform, users are required to send actual money to the MtGox exchange if they want to buy bitcoins over this platform.

I am a customer of MtGox. I bought nearly all of my bitcoins from them. The process was very simple. I went to my bank and started a domestic wire transfer. It didn't take long for the money to arrive at MtGox and be credited in my account there. That was the advantage for me of having this large exchange right under my nose. The MtGox office was located about five minutes walking distance from my university.

At first glance, the statutes above mean that MtGox needs a banking license for accepting actual money deposits. Since they don't have one, MtGox (the company) and its CEO, Mark Karpeles, seem to be in violation of criminal law. Both of the statutes mentioned above come with a prison sentence of up to three years or a fine of up to three million yen, or both, for violations.

3. Banking License Requirements

I am quite sure that MtGox does not have a banking license. But they might apply for one, or someone else might apply for a new banking license with a view to establishing an exchange that will enjoy more customer trust.

Let's have a look at some of the requirements if one wants to receive a banking license. That will also serve as a useful contrast to the rather inadequate protection for depositors provided by the MtGox exchange.

For one, a bank would need to be a stock company (Article 4-2 Banking Act). It needs to have a Board of directors, a Board of company auditors, and an Accounting auditor.

MtGox has none of these.

The minimum capital for a bank is set as one billion yen in Article 5 of the Banking Act, but it can be set higher by Cabinet Order. Article 3 of the relevant Cabinet Order[40] has done this and set the necessary minimum capital at two billion yen.

Article 6 requires that a bank shall use the name "Ginko" (which means bank) in its trade name.

---

[40] k-lenz.de/btc015.

You can't call a bank only "MtGox". That is an excellent way to tell that MtGox does not have a banking license without bothering to check the relevant list published by the Japanese Financial Services Authority[41]. It is a short list with only 35 entries. That makes it very convenient to affirm that, as suggested by the lack of the term "Ginko" in their trade name, they don't have a bank license.

Article 7-2 of the Banking Act requires certain minimum levels of experience for directors of a bank:

"Directors (in the case of a Bank which is a company with committees, the executive officer) who are engaged in the day-to-day business of a Bank shall have the knowledge and experience to be able to manage and control a Bank appropriately, fairly and efficiently, and shall have sufficient social credibility."

I rather doubt that the present director of the MtGox exchange would have a chance to qualify under these requirements.

With these basic requirements cleared, there is another very interesting set of requirements the Japanese Financial Services Authority has set for a bank that operates without physical branches only on the Internet.

---

[41] k-lenz.de/btc016.

These guidelines are published on the website of the Financial Services Authority[42]. Unfortunately there is no English translation available, so I will go ahead and provide a summary below (part VII-1-5 of the guidelines).

They start out explaining their basic stance when thinking about this problem:

Internet banking services are already provided by existing banks. Therefore it is necessary to provide consumer protection by adapting existing regulation and oversight mechanisms to the special circumstances of Internet banking.

Especially for banks that operate without any physical branches, only over the Internet and ATMs, it is necessary that the functions performed in the legacy system by bank branches are performed by an adequate regulatory framework and internal structure of the bank.

For new services made possible by information technology, it is necessary to make sure that the average customer can use them easily and safely.

Considering the aspects above, the Financial Services Authority will, for the time being, apply the

---

[42] k-lenz.de/btc017.

following criteria. These may be reevaluated in discussion with experts and their reports.

a) Has the applicant demonstrated that he has sufficiently addressed the following problems related to the fact that he does not plan to open physical branches:

(1) Reacting to complaints or requests for consultations from customers.

(2) Handling of customers when a system is down.

(3) Obeying the law on requirements for explanations to customers.

(4) Sufficient disclosure.

(5) As measures of preventing money laundering and organized crime, policies of knowing your customer and reporting suspicious trades.

b) When assessing the viability of the business plan: Does the applicant have plans in place if competitors enter the market, the system's technology becomes old, or the environment deteriorates in some other way? Does he have a plan that makes it possible to expect some profit even under such circumstances?

c) Does the applicant have plans to deal with fluctuating conditions, like a massive outflow of customers caused by either the specific fast reaction of the wealthy to conditions like interest, or that it is easy to cease or change transactions?

d) Does the applicant provide a sufficient level of system security? Are there measures in place, including outside expertise, to assure safety? Is there an appropriate plan for dealing with crisis? This must be documented by a report from an independent expert institution.

e) The Financial Services Authority will make sure that the plans and measures the license is based on will be followed after the license has been given, by inspections and by requiring reports.

Now, after this brief summary of these criteria specific to licensing a new Internet bank, let's briefly discuss how the MtGox exchange would do under these.

First off is point a) (1) above. Has MtGox demonstrated their willingness and ability to address complaints or requests for consultations from customers?

No.

They certainly have not.

They have left a guy flying in from London

standing in a cold February snow storm all day. He came all that distance just for the chance of maybe, with luck, actually talking to someone. MtGox held 250 of his bitcoins, worth well over a hundred thousand dollars at the time.

But they left him standing in the snow.

They have left another guy living in Tokyo, with even more funds at risk, sitting all day long on the sidewalk without even once talking to him.

This kind of behavior clearly disqualifies MtGox already from touching any customer funds.

I know lots of people who have tried to talk to MtGox and were completely ignored. I am one of them myself.

The above observations make it also abundantly clear that MtGox is unable to handle customer relations when the system is down, point a)(2) above.

Next I discuss point b), somewhat in advance. I am not aware of any plans MtGox might have if competition enters the market. However, it is safe to say that their market share has gone down substantially in the last year. New exchanges pop up all the time.

Which leads me to an aside remark. If you open the MtGox homepage[43], the first thing you are greeted with is the statement, put in bold and large fonts: **"Trade with confidence on the world's largest Bitcoin exchange!"**

That obviously spells "Bitcoin" wrong, since they are dealing in currency units. It must be spelled "bitcoin" (small b).

But it is also a lie right now. They have not been the "worlds's largest" for quite some time now.

Obviously, that is another way in which MtGox is violating Japanese law. That particular problem is not one of the Banking Act, though, so I will skip a thorough discussion of this point here.

Which leads me back to point a)(3). Has MtGox been obeying the law on requirements for explanations to customers?

Again, **no.**

The above false statement they lead off with on their website is enough to prove that without doubt.

Point a)(4) "sufficient disclosure" is also a complete failure. They have been stonewalling. Mark

---

[43] Found at mtgox.com.

Karpeles, when asked by a Wall Street Journal reporter on the financial health of MtGox, said that information was "confidential"[44].

Well, newsflash for him: If you take $100 million in customer deposits, there is nothing "confidential" about the financial health of your company.

Lastly, a couple of remarks on MtGox system security (point d) above). I am not aware of any third party expert institution report about their practices. Nor do I know enough about the technical side of the Bitcoin network to try such an assessment myself.

I do know, however, that they have been hacked repeatedly, and that the latest problems seem to indicate they have been hacked again. That much is clear.

In contrast, no one has any idea of the amount of damage this may have caused to their financial stability. I don't even know if they have this information themselves.

I also think it is highly irresponsible to run an operation with that much money in bitcoin holdings without even having one single guard at the reception

---

[44] See this tweet by WSJ reporter Takashi Mochizuki k-lenz.de/btc018.

desk.

So, in conclusion, it is quite clear that there is no way MtGox could ever get a license to open an Internet bank if they applied for one in the first place.

That of course means that they should be let nowhere near their customers' money. It also means that their violation of the Banking Act's license requirement is a very serious case.

On March 7, 2014, the Japanese government published an answer [45] to several questions that opposition Member of Parliament Tsutomu Okubo[46] had raised. That answer stated no plans for the government to regulate the Bitcoin network in the future. It was only a short explanation on their point of view on how existing laws apply to Bitcoin.

They note that in their view bitcoins are not a currency. And they think that because of that trading in bitcoins is not banking business under the definition in Article 2 of the Banking Act discussed above. It is only a very short remark without any explanation in detail. But it is an indication that the government thinks, contrary to my point of view here,

---

[45] See Lenz, Japanese Government on Bitcoin, March 7, 2014 blog post, with link to government answer at k-lenz.de/btc044.
[46] See his Wikipedia article at en.wikipedia.org/wiki/Tsutomu_Okubo.

that someone may get away with taking deposits in actual money when running a bitcoin exchange without a banking license.

But what is relevant in this context is the following other short remark in that answer. They say that operating a bitcoin exchange, exchanging bitcoin for yen or other currency, and providing accounts denominated in bitcoin are activities not in the catalogue of business operations allowed under Article 10 and 11 of the Banking Act.

If true, that would mean that someone operating a bitcoin exchange like MtGox could not file for a banking license in the first place. They would need to shut down the exchange the moment they got the banking license.

I think this should not be the last word on this question. I already made it into the New York Times[47] with my opposition to this idea. As quoted there:

If banks and securities firms can't handle Bitcoins, Japanese consumers will be stuck with illegal shadow banks like MtGox, and their risk will be much higher as a result.

---

[47] Hiroko Tabuchi, Japan Said to Be Ready to Impose Bitcoin Rules, New York Tiimes March 5, 2014, k-lenz.de/btc045.

But even if that position of the Japanese government remains unchanged, it is still quite possible for someone who would want to run a safer bitcoin exchange to get a bank license.

All they need to do is set up separate companies for the banking part and the bitcoin exchange part. Banks are not in any way prevented from doing business with a bitcoin exchange.

Set up company A for the purpose of operating an exchange. Set up company B for the purpose of operating a bank. Have bank B issue a guarantee (clearly a transaction allowed for banks under Article 10, Paragraph 2 Number 1 for all withdrawals of both bitcoins and traditional currency funds from the exchange (e.g. the bank will pay out everybody at 100 percent if the exchange company becomes insolvent).

While you are at it, have the bank store the bitcoin paper wallets in a safe, another business clearly allowed to banks under Article 10 Paragraph 2 Number 10. Set access to that safe storage up in a way that guarantees complete transparency on who took out what amount of bitcoins on what date. Do the contract on the safe storage in the name of company A so as to indicate the bitcoins in question are the property of company A, and not some director of that company like Mark Karpeles for MtGox.

One enhancement to this concept would be to have company A act as a "bank agency" under Chapter VII-4 of the Banking Act (Articles 52-36 to 52-61).

The minimum capital requirements for opening a bank agency are very low, only a fraction of the 2 billion yen required for starting a bank. Article 52-38 Paragraph 1 Number 1 leaves it to a Cabinet Office Ordinance to specify that amount. It is set at 3 million yen for natural persons and 5 million yen for companies in Article 34-36 Paragraph 1 on that Ordinance[48].

And bank agencies are allowed to engage in lines of business not enumerated in the Banking Act, if they receive the Prime Minister's approval, Article 52-42 Paragraph 1 Banking Act, which reads:

"(1) A Bank Agent may, in addition to Bank Agency Services and services incidental to Bank Agency Services, engage in other business activities if it obtains the Prime Minister's approval therefor."

Actually, if one argues that running a bitcoin exchange is a "service incidental to Bank Agency Services", there would not be even a requirement to obtain approval. But it would probably make sense to ask for that approval anyway.

---

[48] k-lenz.de/btc047.

The basic idea with this concept: Company A would be subject to some lighter form of regulation and oversight by the Financial Services Authority. That in turn would help to boost customer confidence. For example, Article 52-45 Number 1 of the Banking Act prohibits providing false information to customers, like the false statement at the MtGox website that they are the World's largest bitcoin exchange mentioned already. Article 52-47 requires immediate notification to the Prime Minister, explaining the reasons, if there is a temporary shutdown of business. I recall that MtGox did not explain any reasons when they abruptly shut down their website, and did not notify the Prime Minister. Article 52-50 requires that the Bank Agent files a report on the financial situation of the company each year, which will be made available for public inspection.

There is more, but I will skip discussing any more details. The main point is that once one gets a permission to operate a bank agency business, that comes with regulation and oversight.

The German exchange bitcoin.de uses a similar model. According to their homepage, they are acting as agents for the FIDOR bank. This is their relevant statement:

"Notice pursuant to § 2 Section 10 of the

Banking Act

The Bitcoin Deutschland AG is acting as tied agent of the FIDOR Bank AG within the meaning of § 2 Section 10 of the Banking Act and provides the system of the completion of financial instruments in accordance with § 1a Sentence 2 No. 1 and No. 2 of the Banking Act exclusively in the name and for the account of the FIDOR Bank AG."

Bank agencies are usually in the business of signing up new customers for their principal bank. Get new customers to open accounts. Sell some real estate credit.

With the business model of having traditional money never touch the bitcoin exchange, obviously one needs bank accounts to settle the trades. One could well imagine that a bitcoin exhange required or at least suggested to open a new bank account at a suitable partner Internet bank for the purpose of dealing in bitcoin on the exchange. That would mean new business for the Internet bank concerned. And there is nothing to stop anyone from doing this without actually getting a permission to act as a bank agency yet.

And of course there is nothing to stop anyone who operates a bitcoin exchange to voluntarily comply with regulations required for bank agents, even before they apply for permission.

4. Financial Services Authority

At the time of writing these lines, I still have to find out exactly how the Japanese Financial Services Authority (金融庁) is supposed to deal with illegal shadow banks that take deposits without the necessary license.

I have phoned them twice.

First I talked to their main receptionist and explained that I am an academic studying the Japanese Bank Act's regulation on bank licenses. I was put through to a person who is responsible for bank law there.

I got the opportunity to explain the situation and my interest. The answer was that I should talk to someone else. The person in question was not in charge of enforcing bank law in individual cases, only for researching policy.

My second attempt was phoning a consumer hotline the Financial Services Authority has for accepting complaints about banks or loan sharks from the public.

I talked for a couple of minutes to another

person. I was put on hold. And I heard that there is no one in charge at the Financial Services Authority for this kind of question.

One week later I walked into the Financial Services Authority lobby with one of the MtGox protesters and a journalist from Asahi Shimbun. I thought I might have a chance to actually talk to someone who knows why the Financial Services Authority did not stop MtGox from taking deposits without the necessary license.

That attempt was unsuccessful as well. It did get me a mention in the Asahi Shimbun the next day[49], though. Anyway, I tried.

I had no experience in dealing with the Financial Service Authority directly. When we arrived in the lobby, there was no reception desk, only a line of guards from a security firm.

So I talked to one of the guards. I had printed out an organization diagram and marked the departments I would be interested in talking to, and the order in which I thought they would be relevant.

The day before, Chief Cabinet Secretary

---

[49] Bitcoin, dou naru? MtGox torihiki teishi tsuzuku, k-lenz.de/btc030.

Suga[50] had answered media questions on Bitcoin by saying the Japanese government is collecting information and studying the issue. So I thought I would provide them with some information.

After talking to the guard I was advised to again contact the department that runs the consumer hotline. I already knew that they don't understand the issue from my call to them one week before, but that was all I got.

I phoned them from the lobby, and one guy kindly came down to receive the information I had prepared. That was a copy of my academic paper on Bitcoin law I had published in Japanese in 2013, a draft of this chapter, and a copy of an internal memo from MtGox leaked by the "Two Bit Idiot" blogger[51] earlier that week.

That was more than I could have achieved by just calling them again, so it was a limited success. But I still failed to get a chance to discuss the topic of this chapter with someone from the Financial Services Authority.

They said that they would contact me by phone the next day. For some weird reason they don't seem to be able to use e-mail. And I got a call the

---

[50] en.wikipedia.org/wiki/Yoshihide_Suga.
[51] k-lenz.de/btc031.

next day from someone at the consumer hotline department. Thank you for your information. No, we are not going to comment in any way.

On the evening of that day (February 28), MtGox announced that they had filed a petition to open a "civil rehabilitation procedure". That of course means good news as far as the application of the Banking Law to MtGox is concerned. Even if I had succeeded in talking to the Financial Services Authority, and even if they had moved immediately to deal with the problem, the damage could not have been avoided. It was too late anyway.

I am sure that this failure of communication is due to the fact that I was not able to explain the problem well enough. Sure, if you are talking about regulation of the Bitcoin network, it may be too early for the Japanese Financial Services Authority to have formed an opinion. Regulators world wide are studying the issue and need to come up with a clear framework for this revolutionary new technology.

Eventually, they will do so.

That, however, does not mean that existing law can be ignored, even if it was in no way intended for a bitcoin exchange.

One of those regulations is the requirement to get a license if you accept deposits in actual money.

That requirement does not just magically disappear because you deal in bitcoins.

Many people compare the present state of the Bitcoin network with the state of the Internet around twenty years ago. One example is this recent talk by Jeremy Allaire[52] at MIT (which is well worth watching even if you have no interest in the question of regulation I am discussing here).

Twenty years ago, there was no law specifically addressing the Internet. But of course copyright law, to name only one example, would apply to any copying one did with the new technology as well as any one did with a printing press. As long as there is no legislation introducing specific exceptions to copyright for the Internet space (for example to enable using cache technology in a web server), the old rules apply. The Internet has not magically built a new space where regulation and laws don't apply.

Anyway, back to the Japanese Financial Services Authority.

Eventually, they will study the Bitcoin network. And they will release some specific rules for this new technology. Maybe the Japanese Parliament will eventually enact new rules for Bitcoin in the

---

[52] Jeremy Allaire, What is Bitcoin? And Why Should I Care?, February 18, 2014, k-lenz.de/btc019 (Youtube).

Banking Act.

Until that happens, the old ones apply. And eventually someone at the Financial Services Authority will figure out who exactly in this large institution is supposed to enforce them.

Until then, let's just note one precedent for how the Financial Services Authority deals with violations of the banking license requirement.

That case involved the "Credit Suisse" bank. The Financial Services Authority reported on it (in Japanese) in 2007[53].

In that case, Credit Suisse started a "Japan Desk" department, aiming at the market of wealthy Japanese. And they had one of their employees come to Japan, with the aim of signing up people for the derivative investment products Credit Suisse offered.

The Financial Services Authority took the position that this kind of activity is banking business without a license (taking of deposits). That case also lead to criminal prosecution of the Credit Suisse employee in question for money laundering charges.

---

[53] Financial Services Authority, Credit Suisse no kaigai kyoten ni yoru nihon ni okeru ginkougyou no mumenkyoeigyou ni kan suru doukou ni tai suru yousei ni tsuite, k-lenz.de/btc020.

The Financial Services Authority sent a sternly worded letter to Credit Suisse, demanding that Credit Suisse stop sending employees to Japan and collecting deposits without a license. They also demanded that Credit Suisse study the Japanese Banking Act and take measures to explain these regulations to their directors and employees.

I learn from this that the Financial Services Authority is definitely involved in a case of taking deposits without the license necessary under Article 4 of the Banking Act.

The only thing left to figure out is who exactly in this big institution people are supposed to talk to you when they have information about probably the largest case of illegal shadow banking in the history of this institution.

5. Court Decisions

Let's look at a couple of decisions of Japanese courts, so as to study this issue in more detail.

a) Japanese Supreme Court on Profit Motive

First up is an older decision of the Japanese

Supreme Court. (Decision of the Supreme Court of 26 July 1960). In this case the Supreme Court decided on the question if "taking of deposits" under the Bank Law requires a commercial motive, or if the fact of taking deposits is enough. The Supreme Court took the latter position. Even if you take some deposits without any profit motive, the statute still applies.

In the case of MtGox this problem doesn't come up directly in the first place. MtGox is clearly acting with a profit motive. They take fees for their service and have made some substantial profits from running this exchange.

But this decision still is important. That's because of the reasoning behind it. The Supreme Court takes this position by looking at why there is a license requirement for banks in the first place. In the opinion of the Supreme Court, the reason for this license requirement is that customers of banks need to be protected, and that banks need be supervised, so as to keep trust in the banking system, which is a service in the interest of the public. These reasons make it necessary to require a license even if the company taking deposits is not acting with a profit motive.

The same reasoning could apply as well here. One could say that the reasons for having a license requirement in the first place make it necessary to require a banking license also in the case where those deposits are done for the purpose of buying bitcoins. That is true especially for the aspect of protecting customers.

MtGox has a dismal record in protecting customers. They have unilaterally suspended withdrawal of funds in actual money as well as in bitcoins. They have not disclosed any convincing reasons for doing so. They have stopped talking to journalists. Nobody knows if they still have the funds customers deposited, since they illegally don't disclose the financial statements of the MtGox company, in violation of Article 440 of the Japanese Company Law.

This case is actually an excellent example to show what happens if an underground banking operation like MtGox is allowed to do business. Customers have no idea if they will ever see their money again. Some of them fly in from overseas to protest, as mentioned before. It is a very sad state of affairs. This does not reflect well on the ability of the Japanese regulator to enforce existing statutes.

Back to the Supreme Court case. In short, this case was about deciding between a broader and a narrower construction of the statute. And it takes the broader possible construction, because that is necessary to achieve the purposes of the Bank Law.

This fact is significant, even if in the case I am considering now the question of a profit motive of MtGox doesn't come up directly.

b) Yokohama District Court on International Money Transfer

Next let's look at some lower court decisions where defendants have been sentenced to prison for banking without a license.

First up is a decision of the Yokohama District Court about ten years ago (Yokohama District Court, 25th December 2003).

The defendant in that case was a Chinese citizen who had overstayed his visa in Japan. He received a prison sentence of two years and two months, without suspension, and a fine of one million yen.

There were some other crimes involved (like the overstaying of the visa and forgery of a certificate of alien registration). The part about violating the Banking Act was: The defendant collected 25.6 million yen from customers who wished to transfer money to China and transferred those funds, which is banking under Article 2 Paragraph 2 Number 2 of the Banking Act (conducting of exchange transactions).

The court weighed in favor of the defendant that none of his customers received any economic damages, there were no delays in executing the money transfers, and that the fees he charged were not too high.

The amount of 25.6 million yen in question in this case pales in comparison to the tens of millions of dollars that MtGox has received as deposits. Also, that underground bank operation was only working for about three months. MtGox has been in the business of receiving deposits from customers for several years.

c) Tokyo District Court Decision on International Money Transfer

Next a decision of the Tokyo District Court fifteen years ago (Tokyo District Court, 12 October 1999).

The defendant in that case was sentenced to two and half years of prison and a fine of three million yen. The prison sentence was suspended.

Like in the case above there were some other crimes involved (selling drugs without a license). The underground banking part of the verdict was also about money transmitting, this time to Korea.

The defendant was running a store selling Korean food and the occasional medicine. As a side business he started doing international money transfers to Korea. He collected over 200 million yen over a time span of three and a half months from customers. He then sent the amount to be transferred and the bank account of the customers in Korea by fax to his brother in Korea, who transferred funds from an account in Korea to those customer accounts.

The Tokyo District Court ruled that this is banking under Article 2 Paragraph 2 Number 2 of the Banking Act (conducting of exchange transactions).

On appeal, both the Tokyo High Court and the Japanese Supreme Court confirmed this opinion. (Tokyo High Court 25th May 2000, Supreme Court 12th March 2001).

This might be directly relevant to the MtGox business model. User A located in Japan could transfer Japanese yen to MtGox by domestic wire transfer. Then buy some bitcoins on the MtGox exchange. Then he could transfer these bitcoins in the internal MtGox system to the MtGox account of user B in China. User B could withdraw those bitcoins and change them to cash in China.

What exactly is the difference to the case above where the defendant was convicted for running a money transfer business without the necessary license?

I am not sure right now about the correct answer to this question. I will not examine it in detail right now. That's because under the MtGox business model the fact that they take deposits of actual money is already enough to establish the need for a banking license.

So let's just note in passing that any business model for a bitcoin exchange in Japan needs to think about this decision, and how to avoid getting classified as a money transfer business.

d) Sapporo High Court on Pyramid Scheme

Next up is a decision of the Sapporo High Court from 1978[54].

The defendants in this case set up a pyramid scheme. The court decided that this was a violation of the Japanese Banking Act in place at the time and sentenced the defendants to suspended prison terms.

The court spent some time discussing whether the scheme in question was based on

---

[54] Sapporo High Court Decision October 11 1978.

contracts between the defendants and individual investors only, or if it was based on a contract between all investors, and the defendants were only administering the funds in question in the name of everybody.

Since in the case in question the scheme was based on contracts between the defendants and the investors only, that pyramid scheme meant "deposits of funds" and, for lack of a banking license, was illegal.

That kind of question does not come up with the MtGox business model. Of course all contracts are between the MtGox company and individual customers. There is no contractual relation between customers of the exchange. Actually there is not even a sales contract between individual sellers and buyers, since MtGox is acting as a central counterparty.

It may be possible to set up an exchange based on contracts between all participants. Members of some club or other could agree that everyone invests a million dollars and 1,000 bitcoins, and Member X is trusted with holding these funds for everyone. And then they could start trading with those actual money and bitcoin funds.

In such a case, the bitcoins and actual money deposited would not become the property of Member X at any time. So that would mean there would be no banking license required under the reasoning of the case law discussed above.

On the other hand, this kind of model would only be suited to a club where members trust each other in the first place. If that is the case, there is probably no need for such deposits.

And of course this model probably does not work if you want to open your exchange to a wider audience.

e) Naha District Court on Pyramid Scheme

A similar pyramid scheme case was decided by the Nara District Court in 1995[55].

The defendant in that case was sentenced to one year of prison, without a suspension of the sentence.

The defendant received 31.8 million yen from investors over a time of about one year without having a banking license in one of his pyramid schemes. In another one he received 136 million yen over a similar period of time. In two other cases he received 91 million and 6.6 million yen.

---

[55] Naha Destrict Court Decision July 11, 1995.

The defense in that case claimed that while this looked like a pyramid scheme, it was actually a "moai" scheme [56] traditionally accepted as part of Okinawa culture.

The court was not impressed. In a classical "moai" scheme, the parties are connected to each other by some kind of trust relation in the first place, like family, close friends or colleagues at the work place. The Court cites the Supreme Court decision on pyramid schemes under which those that are based only on contracts between the investor and the defendant are illegal, which I already discussed above. And it finds that in this case there was neither any close relation of trust between the investors nor a contract between them.

When discussing the adequate sentence for this crime, the court mentions that the defendant collected the "vast" sum of 265.4 million yen, and that many of his investors incurred substantial losses.

I don't know exactly how much money MtGox has collected in deposits from customers. But I would be very surprised if the amount in question is not at least an order of magnitude larger than the "vast" sum in question in the case decided by the

---

[56] See the article on the "moai" scheme at the Japanese Wikipedia edition, k-lenz.de/btc11.

Naha District Court.

f) Tokyo District Court on the Definition of "Deposits"

This decision of the Tokyo District Court from 1965[57] is not directly about applying the Banking Act. It is about a tax case.

In this case, a company was founded with the objective of building a shadow bank. Stock holders could deposit funds with the company (of course receiving interest), and other stock holders could receive loans from that capital. All done without a banking license.

As this decision explains, this kind of arrangement was rather popular in the 1950s. There were quite a lot of these shadow banks operating.

The question in this case was if the interest received by stock holders was subject to income tax.

Of course it is. The Court decided as such. But the plaintiff tried to argue that since these were not deposits at a real bank, the clause in the income tax law subjecting interest income from deposits would not be applicable to this case.

---

[57] Tokyo District Court Decision of April 30, 1965.

The Court disagreed with this assessment. And while disagreeing, it noted that the term "deposit" does not depend on there being a licensed bank involved. It is exactly the other way around. The term "banking" depends on whether deposits are involved.

While it is true that in the normal case of banking business the deposits will be received by a licensed bank, obviously there can be shadow banks without a license, which is the whole point of requiring bank licenses and having prison sentences for violations of that requirement.

6. International Standards

I am discussing mostly Japanese law here. But even when discussing Japanese law, it makes sense to have a brief look at how these matters are handled elsewhere.

The reason for that is that foreign law has a lot of influence on the interpretation of Japanese law.

I am going to restrict the discussion to German law and European Union law.

First, let's look what German law says.

In German law, Article 1 Paragraph 1 of the

Banking Law (Kreditwesengesetz) defines the term "bank". Anybody doing banking business for profit or on a scale requiring operations organized like a merchant's.

Banking business in turn is described in a long list in that Paragraph, ranging from number 1 to number 12. Relevant for our discussion here is number 1, which reads:

"The acceptance of funds from others as deposits or of other unconditionally repayable funds from the public, unless the claim to repayment is securitised in the form of bearer or order bonds, irrespective of whether or not interest is paid (deposit Business)." (Translation 2009 by the Deutsche Bundesbank, published at the Federal Regulator Bafin website[58]).

Accepting funds from customers for the purpose of running a bitcoin exchange would qualify under that definition.

That triggers a license requirement in Article 32 of the law. Applicants need to show at least five million Euro of capital if they want to accept deposits. There are many other requirements for applicants to make sure customers can rely on the financial health and responsible management of the newly founded

---

[58] k-lenz.de/btc12.

bank. Details are explained (in German) in a manual published on the regulator's website[59].

Now for some basic information on European Union law. Directive 2013/36 [60] of the European Parliament and of the Council of 26 June 2013 on access to the activity of credit institutions and the prudential supervision of credit institutions and investment firms, amending Directive 2002/87/EC and repealing Directives 2006/48/EC and 2006/49/EC says in Article 9 Paragraph 1:

"Member States shall prohibit persons or undertakings that are not credit institutions from carrying out the business of taking deposits or other repayable funds from the public."

The definition of "credit institutions" is found in Article 4 Paragraph 1 of Regulation 2013/573[61] of the European Parliament and of the Council of 26 June 2013 on prudential requirements for credit institutions and investment firms and amending Regulation (EU) No 648/2012.

That Paragraph reads:

---

[59] Deutsche Bundesbank, BaFin, Merkblatt über die Erteilung einer Erlaubnis zum Betreiben von Bankgeschaften gemaß § 32 Abs. 1 KWG (Stand: 31.12.2007),
k-lenz.de/btc12.
[60] k-lenz.de/btc013.
[61] k-lenz.de/btc014.

"Credit institution means an undertaking the business of which is to take deposits or other repayable funds from the public and to grant credits for its own account."

I won't attempt any analysis or explanation in detail, but it is clear from the above that EU law wants to restrict the business of taking deposits to credit institutions that have the necessary licenses.

7. Interpretation

So, after looking at the Japanese statutes, court decisions involving them, and at German and European law on this issue, let's try to do some interpretation of the Japanese statute.

a) Systematic interpretation

First off, let's try some systematic interpretation. Systematic interpretation means looking at an Article not only on its own, but in the context of the whole law.

Article 2 Paragraph 2 (i) defines normal case banking as "Acceptance of deposits or Installment Savings, in addition to loans of fund, or the discounting of bills and notes". If you walk down the street and find a bank, you would normally expect that bank to take deposits from its customers and lend out that money to other customers in some form or other. They are in the business of receiving credit from their depositors and extending credit to their lenders.

Therefore, the definition in Article 2 refers to both sides of this business.

If that was the only definition of banking, a Bitcoin exchange would not need a banking license, even if they take deposits in actual money and bitcoins from customers, since they don't loan these funds to anyone else.

But Article 3 extends this definition. As already quoted it says (slightly edited for clarity): "Any commercial pursuit involving acceptance of deposits or Installment Savings etc. shall be deemed to be Banking and this Act shall apply."

That means that acceptance of deposits is enough to fall under the definition of banking. The second component of the normal case definition in Article 2 is not a necessary condition.

In contrast, if someone is only in the business of lending money, they are not banking and do not need a banking license. The first component of the Article 2 definition is a necessary condition.

The reason for this is easily understood.

If someone is taking deposits, all customers will be affected if that person disappears or goes bankrupt. If MtGox goes bankrupt, customers world wide will incur millions of dollars of damages as a result.

In contrast, if a lender disappears, that would not be concern his customers. Maybe they could even rejoice in the fact that there is nobody left asking for their money back, and payment of interest.

If a lender goes bankrupt, that does not affect his customers much. They will just pay back their loans and interest to someone else.

That of course means that the need for regulation is much stronger with the "depositing" part of the banking business than with the "lending" part.

Anyway, what Article 3 of the Banking Law clearly says is that the moment anyone takes deposits, they are in the banking business. It doesn't matter if there is anything else involved.

"Sure, I take deposits, but I am also brushing my teeth every day."

That would not be a valid point.

"Sure, I take deposits, but I am also selling

bitcoins."

That is irrelevant as well. As far as this statute is concerned, once you take deposits, you need a banking license.

b) Relation to the Commodity Derivative Act and the Financial Instruments and Exchange Act

Let's try to think about some objections to this view.

One would be to say that a bitcoin exchange is regulated by the Commodity Derivatives Act, and therefore the license requirement in the Banking Act doesn't apply. I have heard exactly this objection multiple times discussing the issue face to face with people.

The Commodity Derivatives Act (商品先物取引法) is Act No. 239 of August 5 1950, and an English translation is available on the Japanese government's law translation website.[62]

There are multiple problems with this objection.

---

[62] k-lenz.de/btc021.

For one, bitcoins are as of now not listed in the exhaustive list of "commodities" this Act is applied to. That list is found in Article 1 of the Cabinet Order No. 280 of August 31, 1950, for which an English translation is available at the Japanese government website.[63]

Next, an exchange under this Act is organized as a contract between all Members of the exchange, while the MtGox bitcoin exchange is based on contracts between MtGox and individual traders. There are no contractual relations even between sellers and buyers of individual trades, since these parties remain anonymous to each other. There certainly is nothing like a contract between all of the over one million customers of MtGox.

It is true that a commodity exchange under this Act can, and in fact is obliged to, take deposits from Members under Article 101 and Article 108. These deposits are different from deposits on the MtGox exchange. They are only guarantee funds that are used if a Member doesn't settle a payment in time. They are not funds used directly for payments, and are not needed in the normal case where all payments are executed in a timely manner.

Even if somehow MtGox could claim a right

---

[63] k-lenz.de/btc022.

to take deposits under the Commodity Derivatives Act, that would of course mean that they would need a license under that Act. They don't have one.

The same reasoning applies if one looks at the Financial Instruments and Exchange Act[64] (金融商品取引法), Act No. 25 of April 13, 1948.

Bitcoins are not listed as financial instruments at the moment. Exchanges under this Act are organized as a contract between Members. Such an exchange has the right and the obligation to take guarantee deposits from Members (Article 114 and 119). But such an exchange would also need a license, which MtGox does not have.

So the idea that MtGox somehow gets to take deposits without a banking license because the above two laws may apply some time in the future to a properly licensed and supervised bitcoin exchange does not seem to have any merit.

c) Comparison to rental agreement security deposits

Another potential objection would be to point out that the deposits on MtGox are there only for the

---

[64] k-lenz.de/btc023.

purpose of clearing transactions with other traders. One could see them as only facilitating payments.

One argument for this point of view would be a comparison to rental agreements. If you rent an apartment, you pay the landlord a security deposit. He obviously doesn't need a banking license for that. The purpose of such a deposit is an advance payment of rent, guarding against default by the tenant.

The problem with this view, however, is that under the MtGox business model there are only contractual relations between individual traders and MtGox. Again, there is no contract even between the seller and the buyer of a bitcoin on MtGox, since these parties are anonymous to each other.

The funds deposited at MtGox are held in their bank account, not in the bank account of some seller or other.

And a landlord is not in the business of collecting funds from a multitude of parties, as MtGox is, to the tune of over one million customers. Also the security deposit in a rental agreement is an advance payment for a contractual obligation already clearly defined at the time of the deposit. In contrast, if someone wires funds to his MtGox account, there is no obligation to pay bitcoins with these funds at that time. Such an obligation only exists the moment the trader buys some bitcoins on the exchange.

In summary, the idea that these deposits are somehow permitted as advance payments like a rental agreement security deposit doesn't seem to have any merit either.

d) Comparison to E-money

One other possible objection would be: Wait a minute, if a bitcoin exchange like MtGox needs a banking license, what about e-money issuers like Japan Rail East, who issues prepaid money cards under the "Suica" trademark? Why would they be allowed to do that without a bank license? MtGox is only taking prepaid funds for the purpose of selling bitcoins to customers, just as Japan Rail East is taking funds for the purpose of allowing customers to use these cards for settling railway fares or other payments (at vending machines for example).

There are several problems with this objection.

For one, it is correct that Japan Rail is taking deposits, and that it does not have a bank license.

However, they do have an obligation under the Payment Services Act[65] to register their business,

---

[65] Shikin kessai ni kan suru houritsu (資金決済に関する法律) ,

and to provide adequate security for the deposits, to guard against consumers being harmed from their insolvency.

MtGox is not registered under the Payment Services Act. And the Bitcoin protocol and network is a peer to peer technology without any single institution (like Japan Rail East for Suica) responsible. Certainly a bitcoin exchange is not in the business of taking deposits in exchange for issuing new bitcoins. They are in the business of brokering sales of already existing bitcoins from sellers to buyers.

For that reason, the Payment Services Act does not apply in the first place to a bitcoin exchange. And even if it did, again, MtGox would be in violation of the registration requirement of that Act, as well as the requirement to provide adequate security.

So this is another objection that does not convince me to change my mind.

e) The Need for Depositor Protection

I have studied this issue in some detail now. I have yet to find any reason why existing prohibitions

---

Act 58 of 2009, k-lenz.de/btc029.

against unlicensed banking do not apply to a bitcoin exchange like MtGox.

But I may be wrong. I may have overlooked something.

For example, Yoshihiro Kataoka argues in an article published in July 2014[66] (in Japanese) that an exchange taking cash deposits does not fall under these restrictions since they are taking them for the purpose of selling bitcoins, though he does admit the possibility of a different result if the exchange in question takes those deposits for longer periods of time without any relation to individual trades (like in the MtGox case).

I am not convinced by that reasoning, but I may be wrong and he may be right. In that case, Japanese capital market law would allow running a bitcoin exchange and taking hundreds of millions of dollars in deposits. We would end up with 28 year old programmers being responsible for keeping those funds safe while lacking clue one about the financial industry.

I think that is not a good idea. And the MtGox case is an excellent example of what happens

---

[66] Yoshihiro Kataoka, Bittokoin tou no iwayuru kasoutsuuka ni kan suru houteki shomonndai ni tsuite no shiron, Kinyuu Houmu Jijyou 1998, 28, 38.

if one does allow this kind of thing. Hundreds of thousands of depositors, most of them not in Japan but in the United States, would end up losing substantial amounts of money.

So if I happen to be wrong in my interpretation of existing law, I think this case would make it advisable to change or clarify the existing statutes, so as to make it clear that, no, you can't just go ahead and collect hundreds of millions of deposits without any prudential requirements. Masayuki Watanabe agrees in a March 2014 short article[67] on how Bitcoin should be regulated in Japan.

Right now, depositors are left standing out in the rain. Or, in the case of the protester I mentioned in the introduction, in a cold February snow storm.

f) Circumvention Clause in the Receipt of Deposits Act

The term of "receipt of deposits" is defined very broadly in this Act. There are two aspects to this.

For one, while there is no definition of the term "deposits" in the Banking Act, the Receipt of

---

[67] Masayuki Watanabe, Bittokoin no kisei no arikata, Kinyuu Houmu Jijyou 1990, 1. See also Masayuki Watanabe, Bittokoin no kisei no arikata, NBL 1021, 7, 9.

Deposits Act gives such a definition. And that definition is very broad. It clearly aims at covering any transaction that has the same economic effect as the simple act of depositing cash in a bank account. As noted above, this definition (in Article 2) is:

"(2) The terms 'receive deposits' and 'receipt of deposits' as set forth in the preceding paragraph means the receipt of monies from numerous, unspecified persons, as prescribed in the following items:

(i) the receipt of deposits, savings, or installment savings;

(ii) company bonds, borrowings or any other thing under any other name with the same economic nature as what is prescribed in the preceding item."

That is interesting for the question whether deposits of bitcoins into an exchange at MtGox qualify as deposits. There is not much doubt possible that wiring cash to someone is a "deposit of money". But one could easily doubt if the same is true for bitcoins.

That's because at this point of the still rather short history of the Bitcoin network, the law in most nations still needs to figure out what exactly they are. Are they a commodity? Are they a currency? Are they a financial instrument? Or maybe we need a completely new category to deal with bitcoins?

No one knows for sure yet.

So there might be an argument that depositing bitcoins at MtGox is not a deposit of money, since bitcoin is not money at this point.

But that argument does only hold for Article 3 of the Banking Act, which lacks the clause preventing circumvention that the Receipt of Deposits Act has.

Depositing 100 bitcoins at MtGox obviously has the same economic effect as depositing an amount of cash equivalent to the price of those 100 bitcoins at the time of the deposit. That's just common sense.

This is important for the application of criminal law sanctions. Both the Banking Act and the Receipt of Deposits Act come with a three year prison sentence. But in criminal law, you can't just apply some statute or other if it doesn't exactly fit the case. There is no room for analogy with criminal law statutes.

Therefore, as far as taking deposits of bitcoins at the MtGox exchange is concerned, that may very well be a crime under Article 8 of the Receipt of Deposits Act but not under the narrower Banking Act.

As noted above, Article 8 Paragraph 3 reads:

"(3) A person who falls under either of the following items is subject to imprisonment with work for not more than three years, a fine of not more than 3,000,000 yen, or both:

(i) a person who violates the provisions of Article 1, Article 2 (1), Article 3, or Article 4 (1) or (2);

(ii) a person who evades the prohibitions set forth in the preceding item, regardless of the name in which or the means by which the person has done so."

In contrast to Article 61 of the Banking Act, this criminal law statute has a clause preventing circumvention. It is intended, like the definition in Article 2 of the Receipt of Deposits Act, to broadly cover any activity that has the same economic effect as depositing cash in a bank account.

Depositing bitcoins in a MtGox account qualifies.

g) Working Around this Restriction

Does that mean that MtGox needs to apply for a banking license or shut down?

I recall that at the recent hearings about future Bitcoin regulation in New York venture capitalist Fred Wilson said [68] that small startups should be allowed some time to grow before they need to comply with the full force of market regulation. A small company with only a few persons involved just doesn't have the necessary manpower and funds to deal with market regulations written with large banks in mind.

MtGox has seen some impressive growth over the last couple of years. They recently announced[69] that they have reached over one million customers. They are not in a stage anymore where they still don't know if they even have a market. It makes sense to require compliance with existing capital market regulations from a large company like MtGox.

That of course makes sense also because with over one million customers, there are more than one million consumers whose funds need protection against various risks associated with depositing money at MtGox.

So, yes, if they don't change their business

---

[68] See Lenz, Growing Up Into Regulation, February 25, 2014 Blog post, k-lenz.de/btc024.
[69] MtGox announcement of December 19, 2013, k-lenz.de/btc025.

model, they clearly need a banking license. And anybody else who wants to start an exchange in Japan would need one as well, if they want to offer their service under the MtGox business model.

As MtGox is concerned, they could of course try to apply for a banking license, and hope that the criminal sanction for their past unlicensed banking business falls short of unsuspended prison sentences. The latter would probably depend upon how much damage to customers they have caused.

One remark aside: Even if MtGox somehow solves their present problems and everybody is able to withdraw their bitcoins again, there has already been considerable damage done. With confidence in MtGox's solvency at a low point, many depositors have sold their bitcoins at a considerable markdown to normal market prices. Right now (February 25, 2014) people are ready to sell about three of their bitcoins on MtGox for one bitcoin not trapped there.

And the part about applying for a license does not seem to have much chance of success. I already briefly discussed what the Japanese Financial Services Authority expects for someone wanting to open an Internet bank with physical branches, and how completely inadequate the MtGox record is compared to those requirements.

That leaves two possibilities. Either they shut down or they change their business model to one that does not involve deposits of either actual money or bitcoins.

The way to do this with bitcoins is very easy. Don't allow customers to deposit bitcoins at the MtGox site. Just require customers to do an escrow transaction with MtGox as the third party for every trade that actually occurs.

The reason that this particular problem disappears very easily with bitcoins is that bitcoin is a far superior technology compared to the legacy banking system or cash. It has the necessary escrow already built into the basic protocol. Applying it to avoid depositing bitcoins at an exchange is very easy with such superior technology.

It is somewhat more difficult with the legacy banking system.

One simple way to avoid any headaches on both sides involving deposits would be to change the business model to one where the buyer sends money to the seller of bitcoins directly, as discussed above.

That would mean that in contrast to the present MtGox model, the buyer and the seller would know each other's names. Trades can't be done anonymously under this business model.

There may be one other way, though I am not sure if it would work right now.

MtGox recently announced for its Japanese customers (I am one of them) a change in the way their accounts are funded.

The previous way of sending Japanese yen to MtGox was by using their central bank account and noting the customer number when doing so. Now they have one account for each customer at their partner bank, JapanNet Bank.

It may be possible to set this up in a way that gives customers the power to withdraw money from these personal accounts themselves, as opposed to waiting for someone at MtGox to process a queue of withdrawal requests.

If that is possible, customers may be understood to have these funds in their own accounts, as opposed to deposited at a bank account under the control of MtGox. That would mean that these funds are no longer deposited at MtGox as far as the Banking Act and the Receipt of Deposits Act are concerned.

In other words, it may be possible to set things up so that the customer as well as the exchange have the power to dispose of the funds in some bank account or other. If that is possible, that may be another valid way to avoid the headaches coming on both sides with a bitcoin exchange having the responsibility of handling customers' funds in large numbers safely.

II. Foreign Exchange Licenses

1. Money Exchange Business

In contrast to the Japanese government, I think that bitcoins are a currency. If so, one of the possible models for regulating a bitcoin exchange would be a money exchange business.

There are several possible variations of that.

One, which I am going to discuss here, is often found at airports. Tourists arriving from abroad walk up to a counter and exchange their currency for the local currency, paying some fee, or getting a rate that ensures a profit for the business operating the exchange.

The most straightforward parallel to that kind of business would be operating a Bitcoin ATM, where people can feed Japanese yen into the machine and get bitcoins out, or vice versa.

In this kind of business model, customers are buying their bitcoins not from other customers at the exchange, but from the operator of the exchange.

There is a definition for this sort of business in the Foreign Exhange and Foreign Trade Act[70], in Article 22-3.

It defines a "money exchange business" as "buying and selling foreign currencies or traveler's checks in the course of trade."

That article requires such money exchange businesses to obtain identity confirmation from customers like banks for internationals payments and keep the identity confirmation records. If they fail to do so, the Minister of Finance may order them to rectify the situation. This does not apply to small transactions as specified by Cabinet Ordinance. Article 11-6 of the Cabinet Ordinance[71] specifies that amount as two million yen.

Assuming that contrary to the position of the Japanese government bitcoins are a currency, that obligation to obtain identity confirmation and keep identity confirmation records would also apply to individuals who are selling or buying larger amounts

---

[70] k-lenz.de/btc039.
[71] Foreign Exchange Order, Cabinet Order No. 260 of October 1, 1980, k-lenz.de/btc077.

of bitcoins in face to face transactions. Or to the operation of an ATM in case of such larger transactions. In contrast, for transactions below this threshold value, there is no requirement to obtain and keep identity confirmation records.

Until 1998, this kind of business was restricted to banks. In 1998 the law was changed and liberalized. Now everybody may buy and sell foreign currencies. There is no need to get a license, or to register the business, as is explained in a FAQ at the Finance Ministry website[72].

That is good news for anybody who wants to open a new bitcoin exchange in Japan.

Even if one assumes with the Japanese government that bitcoins are not currency, MtGox might still have qualified as a "money exchange business".

That's because MtGox allowed trading in multiple currencies. Let's explain that by the example of one of the common ways to use the exchange immediately before it collapsed.

For some time from summer 2013 on, bitcoin prices at the MtGox exchange were higher than at other exchanges like Bitstamp (based in Europe).

---

[72] k-lenz.de/btc075.

That's because MtGox had just about stopped international currency withdrawals. That meant that a lot of users had their dollars trapped in the exchange. The only way to get funds out was to sell those dollars for bitcoins and withdraw the bitcoins (which still worked). That in turn meant that a "MtGox dollar" was worth less than a dollar somewhere else.

So some people used this for arbitrage. They would buy some bitcoin at Bitstamp for dollars, and then sell them at MtGox, at the higher price there. Then they would withdraw those funds to a Japanese bank account, for an instant profit of over 10 percent per arbitrage cycle. You could double your money in two months (taking the counterparty risk of either Bitstamp or MtGox going out of business).

For the discussion here the important part is: Operating a bitcoin exchange with multiple traditional currencies allows customers to change their dollars into Japanese yen, as in the example of the MtGox arbitration.

Therefore, if Japanese law still restricted the money exchange business to banks, like until 1998, people could not operate multi-currency exchanges, even when assuming with the Japanese government that bitcoins are not a currency.

While it is true that anyone can buy and sell

foreign currency in Japan freely, there are reporting obligations. These apply if the amount of currency bought and sold is over one million yen per month, Article 55-7 of the Foreign Exchange and Foreign Trade Act and Article 18 of the Finance Ministry Ordinance on Reports under the Foreign Exchange and Foreign Trade Act[73].

Failing to file that report, or filing a false report is a crime under Article 71 Number 8 of the Foreign Exchange and Foreign Trade Act, punishable by prison with work up to 6 months or a fine of up to 500,000 yen.

The Finance Ministry has published a pamphlet[74] about this reporting requirement, and an FAQ[75] (in Japanese). According to these explanations, this reporting system was introduced in 2005 as an anti-money laundering policy. This is based on recommendations from the Financial Action Task Force (FATF), so as to prevent abuse of money exchanging businesses for the purposes of money laundering.

This may be an interesting reference case

---

[73] Finance Ministry Ordinance No. 29 of March 19, 1998, k-lenz.de/btc078.

[74] Finance Ministry, Gaika ryogae wo okonau katagata he, k-lenz.de/btc079.

[75] Finance Ministry, Gaika ryogae gyoumu.

when discussing future recommendations at the FATF level. Let's find out what exactly the FATF recommends about money exchange businesses.

The last recommendations [76] from February 2012 address money exchange businesses in Recommendation 26. It reads:

"At a minimum, where financial institutions provide a service of money or value transfer, or of money or currency changing, they should be licensed or registered, and subject to effective systems for monitoring and ensuring compliance with national AML/CFT requirements."

Clearly, Japan is not following this recommendation. A 2010 FATF report addressing the money laundering risks of money exchange businesses notes[77] that Japan has neither licensing nor registering requirements for currency exchange businesses. As the 2012 recommendations, this report recommends a requirement of licensing or registering for money exchange businesses (115), reinforcing supervision (116), and making sure that operators are

---

[76] International Standards on Combating Money Laundering and the Financing of Terrorism and Proliferation - the FATF Recommendations, k-lenz.de/btc070.
[77] Financial Action Task Force, FATF Report: Money Laundering Through Money Remiitance and Currency Exchange Providers, June 2010, k-lenz.de/btc81, 47.

fit and proper (117), among other things.

As this report notes at paragraph 44, a license is required for currency exchange services in most countries. That makes Japan a very liberal country for operating currency exchanges in an international comparison. That in turn makes it an attractive destination for startups with limited manpower and financial resources to deal with burdensome overregulation to get to market fast with a bitcoin exchange project.

2. Forex Trade

While it is possible to have only the operator of the exchange sell and buy bitcoins (like in the case of a bitcoin ATM), most exchanges have a different business model. They broker transactions between their customers, for a fee.

And in some cases (for example at the kraken.com exchange), customers can also take positions on future prices.

In the Japanese market for traditional currencies, this kind of trade is called "FX trade". Obviously the "F" means "foreign" and the "X" means "exchange"

In contrast to the money exchange businesses discussed above, traders are not necessarily interested in actually selling or buying foreign currency. Rather their interest is in making a profit if the exchange rate goes in the direction they predict.

This is a risky business. The Financial Services Agency explains[78] these risks like this:

"For one, only operators registered under the Financial Instruments and Exchange Act are allowed to offer this kind of investment opportunity. Investors are advised to check if the operator they are talking to actually has complied with that registering obligation.

"Even when dealing with a registered operator, it is essential to check their credit, and understand the deal proposed well,

"FX trades can result in large profits from small investments. However, they can also result in large losses even greater than the amount invested. They are very risky. It is necessary to understand the risk involved and make an informed decision about investing."

Those operators who are registered also are

---

[78] Financial Services Agency, Iwayuru gaikoku kawase shoukokin torihiki ni tsuite, k-lenz.de/btc082.

members of the Financial Futures Association of Japan[79]. This association presents some interesting information about recent changes in the regulation of FX trades.

One is concerned with how operators handle their customers' money. Of course there is a requirement to clearly separate assets of the operator from assets of their investors. And regulation about this was changed in 2009. This page[80] at the Financial Futures Association of Japan discusses this change in detail.

The reason for this change was that several operators went out of business from the summer of 2007 on. Also the world wide financial crisis in 2008 increased risks associated with "cover trade" partners. For these reasons, the Cabinet Ordinance was changed to impose an obligation to deposit all customer funds with a trust company or a financial institution offering trust business.

Article 143 of the Cabinet Ordinance[81] on the Operators of Financial Instruments Businesses contains these new rules, which in turn are based on

---

[79] See their homepage here: k-lenz.de/btc083.
[80] Financial Futures Association of Japan, Kubun kanri houhou no shintaku ipponka, k-lenz.de/btc084.
[81] Available (in Japanese) at the Financial Futures Association of Japan website, k-lenz.de/btc085.

Article 43-3 of the Financial Instruments and Exchange Act.

It is open to debate if bitcoins are a currency right now. Therefore these rules may not apply to a bitcoin exchange operating in Japan, even if they offer futures contracts.

But it obviously is a good idea to keep customer funds separate from funds of the operator. Anyone operating an exchange in Japan should have a look at these regulations and consider applying them voluntarily to their business model.

There are two reasons for doing so. One is the fact that exchanges can't expect to get large numbers of customers signed up if they are operating in a shady way not worthy of their customers' trust. And the other is that eventually the Japanese government will require some kind of registration or license from bitcoin exchange operators. Once that happens, it will be much easier to clear that regulatory hurdle if the exchange in question can point to a history of responsible management of their customers' funds.

I think the idea of keeping customer funds in a trust company account has so much merit it should even be considered by bitcoin exchanges operating in other jurisdictions, for which these rules don't apply even if one thinks that bitcoins are a currency and they offer futures contracts.

Another change enacted in 2009 is about investor protection by a "loss cut rule". It is discussed in much detail on this page[82] at the Financial Futures Association.

When investing in the foreign exchange derivatives markets, without such a rule the customer risks not only his capital. If things go wrong, he may lose even more than that. A "loss cut rule" is a countermeasure to this unlimited risk. It requires that the operator of the foreign currency futures exchange dissolves a customer position once it reaches an amount of loss specified in advance.

That does not necessary limit the loss to the amount specified. The market may drop even further in the time between the specified loss being reached and an operator reacting to actually dissolve the position. If the operator does not have computer programs in place that react immediately any time of the day but rather relies on human operators to ensure stop loss position dissolving, there may be substantial additional losses.

Anyway, this change was based on Article 40

---

[82] Financial Futures Association of Japan, Loss cut rule no seibi, junshu no gimutsuke, k-lenz.de/btc086.

Number 2 of the Financial Instruments and Exchange Act. That requires operators to conduct their business in a way that is not detrimental to the protection of investors. Article 123 of the Cabinet Ordinance on the Operators of Financial Instruments Businesses specifies the concrete rules for investor protection.

This was changed to include a duty to introduce a system for monitoring stop loss situations, and to actually dissolve positions if such a situation occurs.

Again, this kind of investor protection is probably not yet required from operators of a bitcoin exchange. But it is a good idea anyway. The kraken.com exchange previously mentioned allows customers to set a stop loss target, but does not require them to do so, see their trading guide[83].

The third change was introduced in 2010. It sets a limit for the leverage allowed in foreign currency futures trades, at a leverage factor of 25. That means customers are required to deposit at least 4 percent of any open position they want to take. Again, there is a page at the Financial Futures Association of Japan[84] discussing this change in detail.

---

[83] Kraken.com, Trading Guide, k-lenz.de/btc086.
[84] Financial Futures Association of Japan, Shukoukin kisei, k-lenz.de/btc087.

The risk of futures trades (as well as the chance for big gains) goes up with the leverage factor. This limits the risk investors can take. It is the equivalent of preventing gamblers in a casino from putting everything on one number at the roulette table (large risk and large payout).

I am not sure if this is a good idea. Personally I would not want to take any short term position on the future price of bitcoins. I am convinced that this price will go up when measured in spans of a couple of years. But I have no idea what the price next week or next month may be.

But if someone wants to take such risks, why would the regulator need to limit the risk by ordering a maximum leverage?

I for one don't think that a bitcoin exchange like kraken.com should introduce such a limit voluntarily.

III. Money Transmitting Business Licenses

1. Prepaid Payment Services

There are a couple of statutes that may be

relevant for Bitcoin protocol based business plans, as far as licenses for money transmitting services are concerned.

First up is the Payment Services Act[85], a relatively new law that was enacted in 2009. I was not able to find an English translation at the Japanese government law translation website or elsewhere, so I will need to provide translations myself.

The second chapter of this Act regulates various forms of prepaid payment services (Articles 3 to 36). There are the following two categories.

The first is prepaid payment services for the purposes of accepting money from one's own customers (Articles 5 and 6). I will call them "prepayment services for own purposes" here. The second is prepaid payment services that allow dealing with third parties (Articles 7 to 12). I will call these "prepayment services for general use" here.

Taking the Japan Rail East "Suica" service as an example, if Japan Rail used these cards only to collect fares from their railway customers, that would be a service under the first category. And as far as they allow payment at a convenience store or a vending machine not operated by Japan Rail, that

---

[85] Shikin kessai ni kan suru houritsu, Law No. 58 of 2009, k-lenz.de/btc032.

means they are in the second category.

If you want to operate a prepayment service for own purposes, Article 5 of the Act requires filing a report with the Prime Minister. And under Article 6 the Financial Services Authority publishes a list of companies who have reported under the law. Right now that list has 766 entries[86] (March 2014).

In contrast, running a prepayment service for general use requires registration with the Prime Minister (Article 7). Like in the other category, a list of operators that have registered is published by the Financial Services Authority[87]. It has 1051 entries (March 2014).

Article 10 lists circumstances that would lead the Prime Minister to refuse registration. The purpose of these conditions for registration is to exclude operators that are not trustworthy.

It must be noted at this point that all these prepaid services necessarily mean that customers deposit money with the operator. If you have a Japan Rail "Suica" card and deposit 1,000 yen on that card at a ticket vending machine, Japan Rail has your 1,000 yen, as well as all the deposits of other customers.

---

[86] Available at k-lenz.de/btc033.
[87] Available at k-lenz.de/btc034.

Clearly they are allowed to take these deposits without a banking license under the Payment Services Act. That means that this act is one exception to the general rule that you need a banking license for taking deposits.

But especially if the prepaid payment service in question is for general use, people need to be able to trust the service operator. In other words, depositors in this kind of scheme need to be protected against fraud, incompetence, or bankruptcy of the operator. This registration model provides a minimum of such protection.

Under Articles 14 to 21 of the Act, operators of both types of services need to post security of an amount of at least half of outstanding balances on prepaid service cards. That means that even if suddenly all their funds disappear and they go bankrupt, customers will be able to at least retrieve half of their deposits.

In contrast to these prepaid payment services, bitcoins don't have an issuer. There is no single institution issuing bitcoins, just like there is no single institution running the Internet. That means that miners are not required to register their business with the Prime Minister under Article 7 of the Act.

Therefore I think the Bitcoin network as such

does not fall under the act. Masayuki Watanabe disagrees in a March 2014 article[88], where he proposes treating exchanges as issuers.

I am not convinced by that. Bitcoins are issued by the mining process, not by exchanges. Exchanges are a place to sell and buy already existing bitcoins. Just as a convenience store selling an Amazon prepaid card is not the issuer of that card, MtGox has never issued even a single bitcoin.

But one could very well imagine that one of the over 1,000 businesses active in the prepaid payment space in Japan allows customers to fund their prepaid cards with bitcoins. Or someone could build a new prepaid payment service provider under this Act with a view to receiving funds from customers by using the Bitcoin network.

In that case, they would fall under the Payment Services Act. But that is not because they build their business model on top of the Bitcoin protocol. It is because they provide a payment service. The fact that funding the card in question uses bitcoins has nothing to do with that.

It is also worth noting that payment services providers under this Act need to post security. If the

---

[88] Masayuki Watanabe, Bitcoin (bittokoin) ha gouhou na no ka?, NBL 1018, 7, 9.

MtGox exchange had been under a similar obligation, customers would get back at least half of their funds.

This is one more reason against the theory that MtGox was somewhat allowed to take customer deposits because payment service providers under this Act are allowed to do so. If your business model involves taking deposits from customers, this Act is the only exception from the license requirements of the Banking Act and the Receipt of Deposits Act.

And while it comes with much less depositor protection than with bank deposits, it does not come with zero customer protection, as in the case of MtGox.

2. Money Transfer Business

The Payment Services Act also provides regulation for non-bank money transfer businesses.

As discussed above, Article 4 of the Banking Act requires a banking license for banking business. Article 3 says that taking deposits means banking business (with the exception of the prepaid payment services discussed above). And Article 2 Paragraph 2 says also that the "carrying out of exchange transactions" is banking business.

Looking at Japanese case law, we already found out that money transfer services fall under this clause. Providing payment services is, as a general rule, restricted to banks.

But Article 37 of the Payment Services Act states an exception. Registered money transfer businesses may provide money transfer services, with a limit of up to one million yen per transaction (Article 2 Number 2 Payment Services Act and Article 2 of the relevant Cabinet Order[89]).

That means money transfer businesses need to register under the Payment Services Act. And they are not allowed to transfer more than one million yen per transaction without a banking license.

I recall that MtGox was accused of running an unlicensed money transfer business by the American government and had substantial funds frozen in the process. I discussed this case in some detail in May 2013 on my blog[90].

At the time, I did not agree with the idea that running a bitcoin exchange is a money transmitting business. I thought that MtGox was just a user of money transmitting businesses (like Dwolla at the

---

[89] k-lenz.de/btc035.
[90] Lenz, Seizure Warrant Against Mutum Sigillum, k.lenz.name/LB/?p=9369.

time).

I am not so sure now.

Actually, if you had bitcoins deposited at MtGox, you could withdraw them to any Bitcoin address you wanted (before the withdrawals were stopped, of course).

That means you could fund your MtGox account and then withdraw bitcoins to some third party Bitcoin address to pay them some money. That means customers of MtGox could use it as a money transmitter.

Since MtGox didn't register as a money transmitting business under the Payment Service Act either, they would have been in violation of the criminal law statute in Article 61 of the Banking Act not only for accepting deposits, but also for running a money transfer business. There is no separate criminal law statute for running a money transmitting business without registering in the Payment Services Act. That is not necessary, since Article 37 works as an exception to the license requirement of Article 4 of the Banking Act. Without a registration that exception does not apply, which means that the normal sanction in Article 61 of the Banking Act applies.

There are a couple of ways to avoid this problem.

Obviously, if you don't accept bitcoin deposits in the first place, there is no way withdrawals could go to third parties. And refraining from accepting bitcoin deposits seems to be necessary anyway because of the Receipt of Deposits Act.

But even if you run a business model accepting bitcoin deposits, you could still avoid becoming a money transmitting business with the simple step of allowing withdrawals only to Bitcoin addresses that were used for funding by the customer and are therefore known to be under his control. A customer who did not fund his account with bitcoins would need to prove in some other way that he controls a bitcoin address before being allowed to withdraw bitcoins to that address.

That way of doing things would have the added benefit of making it harder for hackers to withdraw funds to a Bitcoin address the customer does not control as well.

An alternative approach would be to allow withdrawals to third party Bitcoin addresses as long as they are below one millon yen, and register the exchange as a money transfer business under the Payment Services Act. Part of the service provided to customers would be an online wallet in that scenario.

But again, I think it is a bad idea to allow for

bitcoin deposits in the first place. One should try to avoid that, as long as the bitcoin exchange in question does not have a bank license.

3. Electronically Recorded Monetary Claims Act

Act No. 102 of June 27, 2007 is also potentially relevant for Bitcoin in Japan. There is an English translation available [91] at the Japanese government law translation website.

The basic idea of this Act is to provide a service to electronically record claims from a creditor to a debtor, and guarantees for such claims. Such a service would be provided by "electronic monetary claim recording institutions", which are regulated under Article 51 to 85 of the Act.

Starting a business as an electronic monetary claim recording institution requires a designation by the competent minister. There are minimum requirements such an institution needs to meet before receiving the designation (for example a minimum capital requirement), and they are subject to supervision. The Financial Services Authority lists [92]

---

[91] k-lenz.de/btc037.
[92] k-lenz.de/btc038.

only four such designated institutions right now.

Of course bitcoins are not claims that any creditor has against any specific debtor. But one could use bitcoins for the purpose of recording claims. The Bitcoin protocol basically is only a technology for running an electronic register in a peer-to-peer environment. The bitcoin currency is just one of the first applications for that technological breakthrough.

That means that miners of bitcoins don't need to worry about getting a designation under this law. They are not in the business of registering claims.

But in contrast, if some advanced business model based on colored coins wants to provide a service that does register claims from individual creditors against individual debtors, they would need to study this law and get a designation under it.

This may also be an interesting way to get something like a "lesser bank license". One could set up an "electronic monetary claim recording institution", get the designation, and then proceed to offer Bitcoin related services. Or one of the existing designated institutions could start offering such services.

The basic concept of this Act is to get claims on the Internet. This is probably one of the major legal innovations in the Japanese financial institutions space of the last couple of years. I must admit that this idea is far less revolutionary than the Bitcoin network. But this legislation may be one model one might look for once the time comes to build a regulatory framework for the Bitcoin network in Japan. "Recording monetary claims" is already rather close to "recording transactions about bitcoins".

4. Foreign Exchange and Foreign Trade Act

This Act is the basis for capital controls. There is an English translation available at the Japanese government's official translation website[93]. Japan had strict capital controls after losing the war, but liberalized these restrictions gradually[94]. The present system does not require permissions for foreign exchange and foreign trade any more, but the Cabinet could introduce such capital controls under this Act.

Obviously, it is very difficult to enforce capital controls once you have a serious amount of money in the Internet cloud. The Bitcoin network adds the ability of making peer-to-peer payments to the

---

[93] k-lenz.de/btc039.
[94] See the article "Capital flows in Japan" at Wikipedia, k-lenz.de/btc040..

Internet. There is no need to have any intermediary institutions, like banks or credit card payment processors involved in a Bitcoin transaction. That in turn means that even if Japan or some other state decides they want to impose capital controls, they can't just turn to the institutions for enforcing them.

That is mostly a theoretical observation as far as Japan is concerned at this particular time. But it is still an important point worth noting.

In contrast, a regulation of practical importance right now in the Foreign Exchange and Foreign Trade Act is Article 55, which requires residents of Japan to report any payments they make or receive in relation to a party non-resident in Japan.

Note that this reporting requirement also applies for receiving payments directly without an intermediary financial institution involved. The only practical way to do this before the Bitcoin network was to put some banknotes in a letter or a parcel and send that over the postal service or some private company offering similar services.

That becomes clear when looking at Paragraph 2 of Article 55. It says that if the payment in question was made through exchange transactions made by banks, the banks would be filing the reports. That means that otherwise the person who made or received the payment would be required to file the report themselves.

There is a criminal sanction for people who don't report in Article 71 No. 2 (imprisonment with work of up to six months or a fine of up to two hundred thousand yen).

The Bitcoin network is especially useful for international payments. It beats competing payment system like bank wire transfers or credit cards by large margins on cost.

That would change dramatically if people were required to report any such payment to the Japanese government.

Fortunately, if one looks at the Cabinet Order and the Finance Ministry Ordinance[95] implementing this reporting requirement, there is an exception for small amount payments. These are set in the Ministry Order as 3 million yen in relation to North Korea and 30 million yen for payments in relations to all other countries.

But that still leaves a requirement for payments exceeding that threshold to report. Any resident of Japan involved in such a payment needs to file a report with the Japanese government.

---

[95] k-lenz.de/btc041.

This may have consequences for how an exchange in Japan needs to handle bitcoin withdrawals. If it allows, like the MtGox exchange did, for withdrawals to any address the customer specifies, customers could use the exchange for payments. They only need to fill in a Bitcoin address of whomever they want to pay. And if the exchange does not require proof from the customer that they complied with the reporting requirement in Article 55, this may be a problem.

It is a good idea for security reasons anyway to restrict Bitcoin addresses for withdrawals of bitcoins from an exchange to one address belonging to the customer. That way, anyone hacking into a customer's account will be unable to withdraw bitcoins to an address that customer does not control. But this policy would have the added merit that this makes it impossible to use the exchange as a payment service provider. That would seem to remove any possible problems for the exchange from Article 55. It will be the sole responsibility of the customer to follow - or not follow - the report requirement.

On the other hand, if the bitcoins deposited on an exchange are legally property of that exchange, as opposed to property of the customer, one could see the withdrawal as a payment from the exchange to the customer. That may trigger a reporting requirement if such a withdrawal exceeds the threshold noted above.

5. Overseas Wire Transfers Act

The "Act on Submission of Overseas Wire Transfers for Purpose of Securing Proper Domestic Taxation" is another Act with a Very Long and Difficult to Remember Title. I will call it briefly the "Overseas Wire Transfers Act" here. There is no English translation available at the Japanese government official translation website. The Japanese version is published here[96].

Article 3 of that Act requires anyone who does a wire transfer from Japan to another country or receives a wire transfer from overseas to give the bank handling the transaction his name and address, and in the case of a payment to an overseas party also the purpose of the payment. This means that if bank wire transfers are the only way to move money to and from Japan, it is impossible to make anonymous payments.

If someone either does not state his name and address or uses false information, that is a crime under Article 9 of the Act, punishable by prison with

---

[96] k-lenz.de/btc042.

work up to one year or a fine up to 500,000 yen. Since banks will not do a wire transfer without this information, only the second alternative (stating false information) is of any practical relevance.

The Act states as purpose in Article 1 to ensure proper taxation. But this is also a recommendation of the Financial Action Task Force to prevent money laundering. From the text of Recommendation 16 of February 2012[97]:

"Countries should ensure that financial institutions include required and accurate originator information, and required beneficiary information, on wire transfers and related messages, and that the information remains with the wire transfer or related message throughout the payment chain."

Japan is a Member of the Financial Action Task Force. This law is not something specific to Japan, but the international standard.

Article 4 of the Act further requires banks to report to the tax authorities on all international wire transfers over the threshold of one million yen specified in Article 8 of the Financial Ministry Ordinance[98].

---

[97] k-lenz.de/bit33.
[98] k-lenz.de/btc043.

In contrast to the reporting requirement in the Foreign Exchange and Foreign Trade Act discussed above, this reporting requirement does not apply to payments done without the help of a financial institution. That means it does not apply to the situation where someone pays someone overseas over the Bitcoin network. That may change if in the future Japanese banks offer accounts denominated in bitcoins, and the payment is made by using such a bank. Right now there are no such banks.

With a payment over the Bitcoin network, there are no such requirements. If the owner of one or both of the Bitcoin addresses involved is not known to the authorities, the Bitcoin network can be used for anonymous payments, in contrast to the traditional payment over wire transfers.

On the other hand, if law enforcement agencies do know one or both parties of a Bitcoin transaction, they can check this transaction any time they want. The blockchain is a public ledger. Anyone can look at it. With a wire transaction, law enforcement needs a warrant for actually using the data collected under this system.

Right now, this Act does not apply to someone doing a Bitcoin transaction. Customers are required to attach their names and addresses to payments when they are using a bank. Bitcoin payments do not use banks. Therefore, the obligation to state a name and address in Article 3 does not apply.

CHAPTER THREE: TRADING RULES

I. Market Abuse

1. Insider Trading

a) Insider knowledge and the MtGox case

When discussing the MtGox case, there are some questions of insider trading that may be relevant.

One situation is the trade between bitcoins trapped at the MtGox site after withdrawals were suspended and normal bitcoins. There was a site called bitcoinbuilder.com that enabled such trades. People could buy MtGox coins (or "Goxcoins") for normal bitcoins.

There was also a thread at the popular "bitcointalk" BBS[99] where people traded Goxcoins for real bitcoins.

---

[99] k-lenz.de/btc048

Obviously, any trader with inside connections to MtGox would get a massive advantage over outsiders. If they had bitcoins stuck at MtGox, they would get more real bitcoins for their Goxcoins than if their insider knowledge of the impending collapse was already public.

One might say that purely as a question of morals, using such insider knowledge of MtGox problems to score an extra profit should be avoided. It is another question if Japanese insider trading regulations would apply to this situation.

Another possible question would be concerned with arbitrage between MtGox and other exchanges.

For most of the later half of 2013 until about January 2014, the price of one bitcoin on MtGox was between 10 to 20 percent higher than the price at other exchanges.

The reason for this was that MtGox had just about stopped international withdrawals in dollars. American customers who had sold bitcoins on the MtGox exchange and dollars on their accounts there found that withdrawals of dollars to the United States either took multiple months or was completely impossible.

A customer of MtGox in such a situation

would have no choice but to sell his dollars for bitcoins, and withdraw the bitcoins. That of course meant that more people would want to buy bitcoins for dollars, raising the price.

That in turn gave an opportunity for people based in Japan, who were at the time able to withdraw traditional money from the MtGox site within a couple of days. They would buy bitcoins at some other exchange for 600 dollars and sell them at 800 dollars at MtGox, and repeat that cycle.

That arbitrage opportunity offered some interesting returns. People would make 20 percent profit on one such deal, and could repeat the cycle. I have heard from one trader at the Tokyo Bitcoin Meetup who doubled his money in two months.

The only problem with that was that there obviously was a counterparty risk involved. If MtGox became insolvent, as they actually did, customers engaged in this arbitrage cycle could lose all their money.

That in turn means that it was another massive insider advantage for anyone who knew what was going on to time this arbitration to stop exactly a week before MtGox stopped payments. Again, such an insider could secure some massive profits, but without the risk everyone else had.

There are probably many other situations in the early days of the Bitcoin protocol where similar insider knowledge leads to unfair advantages in the market. What has the Japanese statute to say about insider trading?

b) Japanese Statute

The Japanese statute covering insider trading is Article 166 of the Financial Instruments and Exchange Act. An English translation of this law is available[100] at the official law translation website of the Japanese government.

Article 166 is a rather long text. I will skip reproducing it here.

But there are a couple of reasons why this statute is not applicable.

For one, Article 166 is clearly only applicable to trading in stocks. It requires an "insider" to be a director, shareholder, or a regulator that has statutory authority over the company.

If bitcoins were issued by some stock company (they are not), the "CEO of Bitcoin" would qualify as an insider under this statute. But the way

---

[100] k-lenz.de/btc049.

the Bitcoin protocol works, there is no such company. It is a peer-to-peer protocol, exactly like the Internet. Just as there is no "Central Internet Authority" (CIA), there is no "Central Bitcoin Authority" (CBA).

Some people may think that is a weak point of the Bitcoin protocol. I believe the opposite is true. Since there is no central authority, there is no single point of failure. Even if MtGox had still been the largest bitcoin exchange when it went into insolvency, other exchanges could have taken its place. So even large failure of companies vital to the Bitcoin infrastructure are unable to affect the mid-term and long-term prospects of the Bitcoin network in any way.

Anyway, the Japanese insider trading statute is clearly only applicable to stocks, and insiders are only persons on the inside of a company whose stocks are traded. Bitcoin may be a financial instrument (I think it is); but it is certainly not a stock.

That means that under present Japanese insider trading regulations, the cases noted above are not covered in the first place.

It is a different question if there is a need for legislation to change this. But under existing law, there is no case for violation of insider trading regulation for any of the insiders connected to the

MtGox case discussed above.

2. Market Manipulation

There have been some reports on automated trading activity at the MtGox site. An anonymous poster at the Reddit Bitcoin forum reported[101] on such activity. In his analysis, this automated trading activity was supposed to artificially increase market prices.

I am not sure how much one can trust this anonymous source. And, as pointed out in this blog post by Cornell professor Emin Gün Sirer[102], buying in a regular pattern over a longer time like this is exactly what one would do if one wanted to avoid raising the price while investing larger sums in bitcoins.

But at least theoretically, insiders at MtGox may have placed orders for bitcoins while not funding the accounts in question with dollars. Once you have an exchange acting as a central counterparty like the

---

[101] Post about the "Willy Report" from May 26, 2014, k-lenz.de/btc098. The report was hosted at Wordpress, but removed the next day for violation of Wordpress terms of service.
[102] Emin Gün Sirer, Willy and Markus Do Not Prove Market Manipulation, May 27, 2014, k-lenz.de/btc099.

MtGox exchange does, sellers would not know immediately that the buyer is actually not paying anything. Such an exchange could run automated processes that buy up bitcoins, without funding the accounts, and the sellers would be none the wiser about that fact. Of course, that requires avoiding actually paying sellers by stopping international dollar withdrawals, exactly as MtGox did.

So, if something like this really happened at MtGox, would that be illegal market manipulation? To answer that question, the first thing to do is to look at the relevant statute.

The Japanese statute about market manipulation is Article 159 of the Financial Instruments and Exchange Act. An English translation of this law is available[103] at the official law translation website of the Japanese government.

It prohibits certain acts concerning "securities" (有価証券) or "financial instruments" (金融商品).

So the first question is if bitcoins fall under either of these categories.

The definition for the term "securities" is found in Article 2 Paragraph one of the Act, which

---

[103] k-lenz.de/btc049.

lists up 21 cases that fall under the term. I won't name them all here, but only a couple of them, so as to give a general idea. Number one in the list are national government bonds, Number two are municipal bonds, Number five are bonds (issued by companies), Number nine are share certificates (stocks).

It is quite clear that bitcoins are not on this list right now. So bitcoins are not "securities".

The definition for the term "financial instrument" is found in Article 2 Paragraph 24 of the Act. It is broader than the term "securities". All securities are also financial instruments, but there are four categories which fall under the term "financial instrument", but not under the term "securities".

One of them is Number three in the list: Currency.

If one sees bitcoins as a currency, which for reasons explained above I do, then they are financial instruments. The Japanese government disagrees, though. Under their theory bitcoins don't qualify as "financial instruments" under Number three.

Another possible way to qualify bitcoins as "financial instruments" would be Number four. That concerns "assets for which there are many of the same kind, which have substantial price volatility, and which are specified by a Cabinet Order as those for which it is found necessary to secure the protection of investors with regard to Derivative Transactions (or other similar transactions) pertaining thereto".

Clearly bitcoins are an asset. There are many bitcoins. They have substantial price volatility. So what does the relevant Cabinet Order say?

The Cabinet Order is available (in Japanese)[104], and it says nothing about bitcoins at the time of the writing of these lines.

That in turn means that under Japanese law, bitcoins are not "financial instruments".

Therefore, the rules in Article 157 of the Act do not apply to market manipulation involving bitcoins.

That is different from the situation in Germany. The German regulator BAFin sees bitcoins as "financial instruments"[105].

---

[104] k-lenz.de/btc100.
[105] Bundesanstalt für Finanzdienstleistungsaufsicht (BaFin), Merkblatt: Hinweise zu dem Gesetz über die Beaufsichtigung von Zahlungsdiensten (Zahlungsdiensteaufsichtsgesetz-ZAG), Stand Dezember 2011, k-lenz.de/bit13, 4b).

II. Money Laundering

There are two statutes relevant to money laundering.

One is the Act on Prevention of Transfer of Criminal Proceeds (Act No. 22 of 2007) (Criminal Proceeds Act). There is no translation yet of this Act at the Japanese government's official law translation site, but the National Police Agency has published an English translation[106].

The other one is the Act on Organized Crimes and Control of Crime Proceeds (Act No. 94 of 1991)(Organized Crime Act). This one also is not yet translated on the Japanese government's official law translation website. But the OECD provides[107] an English translation.

The Criminal Proceeds Act is mainly concerned with financial institutions. It requires "know your customer" procedures and reports of suspicious activities. The Criminal Proceeds Act was recently amended. That is because the 2008 FATF evaluation report on Japan[108] concluded:

---

[106] k-lenz.de/btc066.
[107] k-lenz.de/btc067.
[108] Financial Action Task Force, Third Mutual Evaluation Report, Anti-Money Laundering and Combating the Financing of Terrorism, Japan, 2008, k-lenz.de/btc095.

"The preventive system, which applies to a full range of financial institutions and designated non-financial businesses and professions, only addresses customer identification. It is strongly recommended that Japan fully implement the CDD obligations and the requirement to establish adequate internal control".

To address these problems, Law No. 31 of 2011 [109] changed the Criminal Proceeds Act, and introduced new requirements to ask for and record information, like the purpose of the transaction in question or the occupation of the customer. For a detailed discussion of these questions I recommend the recent book by Yuji Katsuki[110] on the matter. Also, as is apparent from the table on page 9 of another recent publication[111], Japan has not followed all of the FATF recommendations in this reform.

The Organized Crime Act has some similar provisions as well, but it also contains criminal sanctions against people involved in money laundering, and a long section on confiscation of

---

[109] Available (in Japanese Language) at the website of the Japanese National Police Agency, k-lenz.de/btc096.
[110] Katsuki, Yuji, Hayawakari kaisei hanshuuhou to torihikiji kakunin no poinuto, 2013.
[111] Gaikoku Kawase Kenkyuu Kyoukai (Study group on foreign payments), Kaisei hanshuuhou no chishiki to taisaku, 2013.

money laundered funds.

1. Criminal Proceeds Act

Article 2 Paragraph 2 of the Act defines the term "specified business operator", which refers to the financial institutions that need to comply with the requirements of the Criminal Proceeds Act. This is basically a list with 43 entries. None of them is "bitcoin exchange". Therefore, when Member of the House of Councilors Tsutomu Okubo asked the government if someone running a bitcoin exchange has obligations under anti-money laundering law, the answer by the government was that they don't know exactly.

Especially Number 33 in that list needs some discussion. It reads:

"Person who trades in currency exchange (which means commercial trading of foreign currencies (which means currencies other than Japanese currency) or traveler's checks)."

The Japanese government thinks that bitcoins are not a currency. I disagree, as discussed above. If one sees bitcoins as a currency, then running a bitcoin exchange falls under this definition, just like running a booth at the airport where one changes Japanese yen for dollars or euros.

As a customer of MtGox, I recall that I did not need to verify my account when I registered first in April 2013. That changed. In summer 2013, verification was required. I sent them scans of personal documents proving my identity and had my account verified.

If the opinion of the Japanese government was correct, MtGox introduced this policy not because they were required to do so under Japanese law, but as a voluntary self-regulation scheme. Obviously, someone running a bitcoin exchange can decide to verify accounts voluntarily.

As a matter of policy, I don't think it makes any sense to leave bitcoin exchanges out of the list of "specified business operators".

The Bitcoin network is less useful for money laundering than traditional options like cash or wire transfers.

That's because with the Bitcoin network, all transactions are by definition recorded in the blockchain. Those records stay there forever, and they are public. Anyone, including law enforcement, can look at these records any time they want. In contrast, if law enforcement wants to look at bank records, they need a subpoena. And if they want to look at cash transaction records, they are out of luck in most cases, since such records may not exist in the first place.

On the other hand, the Bitcoin protocol does not have a field noting the owner of a bitcoin. It is designed to be pseudonymous.

That may seem to make Bitcoin attractive for the purpose of money laundering. It actually is, as long as the connection between a Bitcoin address and its owners can be kept secret from law enforcement.

But there are a lot of weak points. For one, people who want to keep their identity secret from law enforcement when using Bitcoin need to know what they are doing. One small mistake somewhere is enough to tie an address to an individual. It is possible to achieve anonymity even against the considerable powers of law enforcement. But it certainly is not easy.

Law enforcement may have undercover agents in criminal organizations who have access to the information tying Bitcoin addresses to individual criminals. They may strike a deal with someone they arrested to disclose such information in return for a more lenient sentence.

And they may watch with interest transactions from and to such an address without informing the criminal owning it that they are watching, while he thinks that he is acting anonymously. That state of affairs is ideal for the purpose of law enforcement. They know that they can watch, but the criminal thinks he's acting anonymously. That ideal state can't be reached with the bank system in Japan. Since all participants need to be identified under "know your customer" rules, no criminal will think he is anonymous when using a bank. With Bitcoin, a criminal might think he is anonymous while law enforcement is watching.

For these reasons, Barry Silbert claims that law enforcement personnel he has talked to actually want criminals to use Bitcoin instead of cash or wire transfers, as I discussed on my blog[112] in December 2013.

That said, Bitcoin is a superior way of payment and storing value. It is a currency superior to anything we have had before. Therefore, eventually it will become mainstream. For that to happen, it can't insist on shutting law enforcement and money laundering rules out.

While it is still open to debate if someone running a bitcoin exchange is a "specified business

---

[112] Lenz, DEA and FBI Want Crooks to Use Bitcoin, k-lenz.de/btc068.

operator" under the Criminal Proceeds Act, it is clear that in the future they will fall under money laundering rules. And it is a good idea, in my opinion, to voluntarily follow "know your customer" rules already now, even if the legal obligation to do so is not exactly clear right now.

If a bitcoin exchange qualifies as a "specified business operator", they need to collect customer identification records under Article 4 of the Criminal Proceeds Act. They need to store transaction records for seven years under Article 7 of the Criminal Proceeds Act. They need to report suspicious transactions to the competent administrative agency under Article 9 of the Criminal Proceeds Act. A competent administrative agency can require reports from the exchange under Article 13, conduct on-site inspections under Article 14, and provide guidance and advice on compliance under Article 15 of the Criminal Proceeds Act.

Japan is a Member State of the Financial Action Task Force[113]. That means Japan follows the international standards of anti-money laundering policy developed at this international forum.

As of now, there is no international policy recommendation from the Financial Action Task

---

[113] Financial Action Task Force, Japan, k-lenz.de/btc069.

Force about how to deal with bitcoin exchanges. The last recommendations[114] date from February 2012, when the market capitalization of the whole Bitcoin network was still very small. They don't mention Bitcoin in any way.

Even now the market capitalization of the Bitcoin network is only less than $8 billion, according to the coinmarketcap.com website. In contrast, world wide money laundering volume is estimated at $1.6 trillion[115]. The Bitcoin network's market capitalization is less than half a percent of that. Even if all bitcoins in existence were used exclusively for money laundering purposes, that would not have much of an influence on the big picture.

However, Bitcoin is being discussed at the Financial Action Task Force level right now. The latest plenary in February 2014[116] announced that they are "continuing to conduct research on the use of virtual currency and will consider whether further policy measures are needed." The Financial Action

---

[114] International Standards on Combating Money Laundering and the Financing of Terrorism and Proliferation - the FATF Recommendations, k-lenz.de/btc070.
[115] FINCEN Director Jennifer Shasky Calvery, Prepared Remarks at the Association of Certified Anti-Money Laundering Specialists (ACAMS) 19th Annual Conference, March 18, 2014, k-lenz.de/btc071.
[116] k-lenz.de/btc072.

Task Force is expected[117] to publish a paper on the issue later in 2014. And that paper, a very preliminary report, has actually been released in June[118].

Eventually there will be an international standard to stop criminals from abusing Bitcoin. I would be surprised if such an international standard would not require bitcoin exchanges to follow the same due diligence standards that other financial institutions need to comply with.

2. Organized Crime Act

While the Criminal Proceeds Act requires financial institutions to keep out bad actors, the Organized Crime Act provides penal law sanctions for criminals who abuse the financial system for money laundering. I will limit the discussion of this Act here to Articles relevant to running a bitcoin exchange.

First Article 11. Under that Article, it is a

---

[117] Remarks From Under Secretary of Terrorism and Financial Intelligence David S. Cohen on "Addressing the Illicit Finance Risks of Virtual Currency", March 18, 2014, k-lenz.de/btc073.

[118] Financial Action Task Force, Virtual Currencies, Key Definitions and Potential AML/CTF Risks, k-lenz.de/btc105.

crime to knowingly receive crime proceeds. That means that any exchange will need to refuse to do business with criminals knowingly. Under the Act, "crime proceeds" includes revenue from illegal gambling sites (See 2 H of the Schedule listing crimes that trigger application of this Act). If a bitcoin exchange takes money or bitcoin deposits from such a site, they would be in violation of Article 11.

Article 11 is not restricted to "specified business operators" like the compliance requirements in the Crime Proceeds Act. Anyone can commit that crime. For example, if you run some free online service or other like an online wallet, you can't take advertising revenue from an illegal gambling site without violating Article 11.

I recall that the blockchain.info online wallet service took advertisements from the satoshidice.com gambling website. But they stopped that early in 2014. If they had continued taking those advertising funds, that would have come with a considerable risk of violating the Organized Crime Act.

Article 54 earlier required "financial institutions or the like" to report on suspicious activities. If they suspect that their customers may be engaged in money laundering under this Act, they needed to file a report. But that Article has been deleted (it is still contained in the English translation mentioned above, but not in the Japanese original[119]).

---

[119] k-lenz.de/btc074,

CHAPTER FOUR: TAX LAW AND CRIMINAL LAW

I. Tax Law

1. Capital Gains

The value of bitcoins has grown considerably over the last couple of years. One famous example of this is the pizza story. It is documented in a famous thread on the bitcointalk.org site[120].

In May 2010, only about four years ago at the time of this writing, one of the first real world trades involving bitcoins was done. People were discussing the Bitcoin network online, and one of these people offered some bitcoins in exchange for two pizzas.

He got someone to order him those pizzas. And paid 10,000 bitcoins in exchange, which was at the time worth around 41 dollars.

Since bitcoins are trading around $630 as I am writing these lines, those 10,000 bitcoins are worth

---

[120] k-lenz.de/bit41.

about $6.3 million.

I don't know if the other party to that transaction still has those 10,000 bitcoins. But obviously with that kind of explosive price growth, some people will have made significant gains from investing in bitcoins.

And I for one don't think present prices are the end. The Bitcoin network is still growing exponentially every day. Since the price of bitcoins depends on the development of the network, there is still more of the same ahead over the next couple of years.

Anyway, for taxation purposes, the question is what happens with these capital gains. There is no uniform answer that applies in all countries.

In Germany, Article 23 of the Income Tax Act (Einkommensteuergesetz) says that capital gains from everything except real estate are tax free if the gain in question was achieved over a period of more than one year. That means that people holding bitcoins for longer than one year pay zero capital gains tax in Germany. That's actually rather attractive in an international comparison. People holding a lot of bitcoins since the very early days may even want to consider moving to Germany for the purpose of taking advantage of that.

In contrast, the Japanese Income Tax Act[121] (shotokuzeihou, 所得税法, English translation only partially available on the government translation website) gives only a reduced rate of capital gains taxation, and only after holding the bitcoins for five years. Articles 33 and 22 of the Act say that capital gains are taxed as normal income, at whatever rate the taxpayer in question pays. And after holding an asset for over five years, only half of the capital gains are regarded as income.

There is also a tax-free threshold of 500,000 yen per year (Article 33 Paragraph 4 Income Tax Act). That means that taxpayers won't have to worry about declaring capital gains for each transaction buying a cup of coffee with bitcoins, even if the bitcoins in question have gone up in value. The tax office is only concerned with larger amounts of capital gains.

In contrast to capital gains on bitcoins, capital gains from investing in real estate are taxed at a fixed rate of 20.315 percent, if the real estate has been held for more than five years.

For bitcoins, the rate of taxation depends on what other income the taxpayer has. That in turn means that it may make sense for some people to delay realizing capital gains until after retirement to

---

[121] k-lenz.de/btc051.

take advantage of lower income tax rates.

Capital gains from bitcoins are realized if the taxpayer sells those bitcoins for traditional money. But if the taxpayer uses the bitcoins to buy something, these gains are realized as well[122]. It would obviously not make any sense to tax a person that sells half a million dollars of bitcoins and uses that money to buy some real estate, but not tax that same transaction if that person buys the real estate with bitcoins in the first place.

2. Consumption Tax

Japan has a consumption tax of 8 percent. That tax rate has applied since April 2014, up from 5 percent before then.

It is not yet quite clear how Bitcoin will be treated under this tax. There are several different scenarios.

a) Using bitcoins as payment

For one, consider a customer at some online

---

[122] National Tax Administration, Basic explanation of capital gains (in Japanese), k-lenz.de/btc052.

store that buys a camera with bitcoins. Obviously, if he paid with yen instead, there would be a consumption tax of 8 percent to pay on whatever the price of the camera was.

Does paying with bitcoins mean that this consumption tax does not apply?

The relevant law is the Consumption Tax Act of 1998[123], for which a translation is not available on the Japanese government official translation site.

Article 28 Paragraph 1 of that Act says that the basis for determining the amount of consumption tax is the price paid, either in money or in things other than money, and other economic advantages. This is a very broad standard. Clearly receiving bitcoins falls at the very least under receiving "other economic advantages".

Therefore, anyone accepting bitcoins as payment in an online store will have to pay consumption tax for the sales just like if he only accepted traditional currency.

b) Selling bitcoins to a customer

Another question would be what happens if

---

[123] Act No. 108 of 1998, k-lenz.de/btc088.

someone operates a bitcoin exchange where he sells bitcoins to customers himself, as opposed to brokering sales between customers of the exchange. Operating an ATM would be one way of doing this. Does he need to pay 8 percent consumption tax for whatever prices he gets paid for the bitcoins?

The answer to that question is not as clear as the answer to the last question.

One relevant Article is Article 6, which states that everything listed in Table 1 is not subject to consumption tax. And Number 2 of that Table exempts all "means of payment" as defined in Article 6 Paragraph 1 Number 7 of the Foreign Exchange and Foreign Trade Act[124]. That means that selling foreign currency in an exchange booth or with an ATM is exempt from consumption tax.

The definition in the Foreign Exchange and Foreign Trade Act in full reads like this:

"The term 'means of payment' shall mean the following:

"(a) Banknotes, government money bills, small money bills, and coins

"(b) Checks (including traveler's checks), bills

---

[124] k-lenz.de/btc039.

of exchange, postal money orders, and letters of credit

"(c) Economic value inputted in vouchers, electronic equipment, or other objects (referred to as 'Vouchers, etc.' in Article 19, Paragraph 1) by electromagnetic devices (meaning electronic means, magnetic means or other means that are imperceptible by humans), which may be used for mutual payment among unspecified or many persons (limited to those of which the status of use is specified by Cabinet Order as approximate to that of a currency)

"(d) Those specified by Cabinet Order as equivalent to those listed in (a) or (b)."

The Article 2 Paragraph 1 (ii) of the Cabinet order[125] specifies:

"Those which are similar to any of those listed in (a) or (b) of Article 6 Paragraph 1, item (vii) of the Act or in the preceding item, which may be used for payment."

Looking at the above definition, especially item (c) is very close to recognizing bitcoins as "means of payment". Bitcoins have economic value.

---

[125] English translation available at Japanese government official translation website, k-lenz.de/btc097.

They are inputs to electronic equipment or other objects (for example paper wallets). They may be used for mutual payment among unspecified or many persons. And contrary to the definition of prepaid services under the Payment Services Act, there is no requirement of having a central issuer in this definition.

However, item (c) also requires that the Cabinet Order specifies bitcoins as means of payment. That has not happened yet.

While item (ii) of the Cabinet Order cited above leaves some room to recognize "means of payment" similar to those specified in the Act, that is restricted to means of payment similar to those listed in items (a) and (b) of the act. Item (c) of the Act is not referenced in the Cabinet Order.

So for the time being, bitcoins are probably not "means of payment", which means that the exception under Number 2 of Table 1 of the Consumption Tax Act does not apply.

One of the questions by Member of Parliament Okubo to the Japanese government was exactly this. The answer from the government was not very clear.

So it is quite possible that the Japanese tax authorities might require a payment of consumption tax for bitcoins sold from an ATM, or from an exchange under a model where the exchange sells directly to customers, as opposed to only brokering trades between customers.

This would not make much sense. Clearly the spirit of exception Number 2 in the Table 1 listing exceptions from the obligation to pay consumption tax is to except all "means of payment", including those that are similar in function to those listed in the definitions. And if there is anything that should be recognized by Cabinet Order under item (c), bitcoins would be the first candidate.

Maybe the Cabinet Order should be amended to include bitcoins under item (c) in the future, so as to remove uncertainty in this field. If that does not happen, it will be very difficult for an exchange to directly sell bitcoins to customers in Japan. They would be stupid to buy the bitcoins in Japan and pay 8 percent in consumption tax. They would prefer to go to some exchange based in another country.

For example the United Kingdom announced in March 2014[126] that there would be no value added tax (VAT) obligation for the value of the bitcoins if some exchange sold bitcoins for dollars or pounds. I

---

[126] Eric Calouro, HMRC of United Kingdom Issues Tax Brief on Bitcoin, March 3, , 2014, k-lenz.de/btc089.

think this is a sensible position. And anyway, if Japan decides otherwise and requires payment of consumption tax, Japanese residents will buy their bitcoins in London, and Japan will fall back in the race to develop a strong Bitcoin industry.

c) Brokering bitcoin trades

In contrast to the case discussed above, what about the case of an exchange that operates like MtGox and doesn't sell any of its own bitcoins to its customers, but is only brokering sales of bitcoins between customers of the exchange?

In that case, even if one thinks that selling bitcoins should trigger consumption tax for the value of the bitcoins, most of the trades would still be tax free because the seller is not a business. As long as private citizens are trading as part of managing their private investments, consumption tax would not apply.

Of course there may be sellers who are acting as part of their business. For example, if some business takes bitcoins as payments and immediately sells them for traditional currency to avoid any volatility risks, this consideration would not apply. In that case, again, the business would be very stupid to use an exchange based in Japan and pay an extra 8 percent to the government. That would wipe out all the savings over other payment methods that accepting bitcoins brings. They would go to London to sell their bitcoins.

While I don't think Japan should tax the value of bitcoins sold at an exchange, I would have no problem with taxing the fees the exchange charges its customers. These fees are paid in exchange for the service of the exchange (matching sellers and buyers). This service as such is not a sale of "means of payment". And the fees are usually much less than one percent of the trade value. For example, the last exchange I used after MtGox went down is kraken.com. They charge a maximum of 0.2 percent[127] for trades between bitcoins and Euros. Increasing that cost by 8 percent has not much influence on the big picture. I don't think many people would avoid trading in Japan because of such a tax burden.

3. Reporting Duty

The "Overseas Wire Transfers Act" (Japanese version published here)[128] has recently been amended to require Japanese residents to report to the tax authorities if they hold assets worth more than 50

---

[127] Kraken.com, Fees, k-lenz.de/btc090.
[128] k-lenz.de/btc042.

million yen outside of Japan on December 31 of each year (Article 5). From 2015 on, failing to file such a report will be a criminal offense, Article 10 (not yet in force).

The National Tax Agency has published an FAQ[129] on this new reporting requirement. It explains in detail for all sorts of assets how they are valuated and reported. But bitcoins are not listed in that FAQ.

The basic idea behind this reporting requirement is to stop people from hiding their assets from the tax authorities. It applies also for assets that do not generate any income. And bitcoins may look like an attractive option for someone who wants to hide assets from the tax authorities, from his wife, or from his creditors.

I recall that Member of the House of Councillors Tsutomu Okubo asked the Japanese government if bitcoins need to be included in such a report in March 2014, see my translation of his questions above.

The answer to that question depends on the question if bitcoins are an "asset outside of Japan".

---

[129] National Tax Agency, Kokugai zaisan choushou no teishutsu seido (FAQ) (FAQ on the requirement to file a report on assets outside Japan, November 2013, k-lenz.de/btc060.

Where exactly is the location of bitcoins?

I recall having discussed exactly this question in February 2014 at the Reddit "Bitcoin" forum[130]. At that time I was thinking of estate taxes (which State gets to tax bitcoins as assets if the holder dies). But the exact same question needs to be answered here.

With real estate, the answer is easy. You just look at where the real estate in question is. With stocks, there may be more alternatives. You could either ask where the company in question is located, or look at the place of residence of the owner.

If one thinks of bitcoins as an entry in a ledger, one might argue they are located everywhere a bitcoin node is running. That would be great news for governments, since every State could claim that they can tax them for estate tax purposes.

I don't think that would make much sense. Instead, one should look at where the private key controlling a Bitcoin address is located. To do that, it is necessary to distinguish several different ways of holding such a private key.

One is the case of a so called "brain wallet". The holder selects some password he is able to keep

---

[130] Lenz, Where are bitcoins (for inheritance tax purposes), k-lenz.de/btc061.

in memory for the long term. He then uses this to generate a Bitcoin address. If done correctly, this leaves attackers with no way to find out the private key, except asking the holder.

In that case, the location of the private key for tax purposes would seem to be the residence of the owner. For the question at hand here that would mean that the bitcoins would be located in Japan and therefore not "assets located outside Japan".

Another safe way to hold bitcoins is to print the private keys on a piece of paper (paper wallet). In that case, the location of that piece of paper should be decisive. If someone prints his private keys on such a paper wallet and then puts the paper wallet into a safe deposit box of a bank located in Japan, those bitcoins would not be "assets located outside Japan".

Another alternative way of holding bitcoins is to record private keys on some electronic memory device (USB-sticks, hard disks, personal computers etc). In such a case the location of the device in question should be decisive. So if someone stores his bitcoins on a USB-stick and puts that into a safe deposit box of a bank located in Japan, again, those bitcoins would not be "assets located outside Japan".

Yet another way of holding bitcoins is

depositing them at some online service. For example, if a resident of Japan deposits bitcoins at an exchange located in Europe or the United States, those bitcoins would arguably be "assets located outside Japan".

It is not a good idea to leave larger amounts of bitcoins deposited at an exchange. As the MtGox case clearly shows, these exchanges can go out of business very fast and without warning. And as far as the reporting requirement discussed here is concerned, such a move comes with the additional disadvantage of possibly triggering a reporting requirement under this law.

A similar reporting requirement is based on Article 232 of the Income Tax act. It requires taxpayers that have over 20 million yen of income to file a report on their assets and liabilities.

Holding bitcoins can mean substantial assets. Many of the early adopters have become millionaires. So these assets should be part of such a report, if the report is supposed to give an accurate picture.

And since in this case it doesn't matter if the asset is located inside or outside of Japan, the above question of where exactly a bitcoin is does not come into play in the first place. Anybody above the income threshold needs to report their bitcoins just like any other asset.

4. Estate and Gift Tax

The Japanese Estate and Gift Tax Act is not translated at the official government translation website. The Japanese version is published here[131].

Tax rates are different for estate tax and gift tax. For estate tax, the rates are laid down in Article 16. The highest tax rates are 50 percent for everything above 300 million yen. The other brackets are over 40 percent for everything above 100 million yen, 30 percent for everything above 50 million yen, 20 percent for everything above 30 million yen, 15 percent for everything over 10 million yen, and 10 percent for everything else.

These numbers need to be adjusted for a tax-free bracket of at least 60 million yen under Article 15. That applies if there is only one heir. For multiple heirs, every additional heir adds another 10 million yen to the tax-free bracket. In a case with four heirs, there would be no estate tax if the value of the estate does not exceed 90 million yen.

The gift tax has the same tax rates (from 10 to 50 percent) under Article 21-7, but the thresholds are much lower. Everything under 2 million yen is taxed

---

[131] Act No. 5 of Mrch 30, 1950, k-lenz.de/btc091.

at 10 percent. The next brackets are 3 million yen (15 percent), 4 million yen (20 percent), 6 million yen (30 percent), 10 million yen (40 percent), and everything above 10 million yen (50 percent). These amounts need to be adjusted for a tax-free amount of only 600,000 yen under Article 21-5.

Article 1-3 states that Japanese estate and gift tax applies in the following cases. If the heir or recipient of a gift is a Japanese citizen and has had his residence in Japan sometime in the last five years; if the deceased or donor has his residence in Japan at the time of the death or the gift; and if the property in question is located in Japan.

Article 10 has detailed rules of locating property. For example, stocks are located at the seat of the company in question (Number 8), and copyright is located at the seat of the publisher (Number 11).

There is no mention of bitcoins in that list at the time of writing. And none of the items on the list seem to apply. The closest would be "deposits at financial institutions" under Number 4. As discussed in detail above, depositing bitcoins at an exchange like MtGox may be viewed as a "deposit". And I see no reason to treat such a deposit differently from a deposit in yen at some bank or other for tax purposes.

In contrast, Number 4 does not list contents of a bank safe. If someone rents a bank safe from a bank located in Japan and has bitcoins in paper wallet form there, they would not be treated as located in Japan under Number 4.

As far as bitcoins are not located in Japan under Number 4, under Article 10 Paragraph 3 the residence of the deceased or donor would determine the location of the bitcoins.

If the deceased or donor has a residence in Japan, Japanese estate and gift taxes are due already under the second case of Article 1-3.

II. Criminal Law

1. Stealing Bitcoins and the Japanese Theft Statute

a) Theft

There are reports that MtGox lost 744,408 bitcoins to theft. I got this number from an internal document leaked in February 2014 and published here[132].

That development makes it of interest to have a look at the theft statute of the Japanese Penal Code. The Japanese government provides an English translation of that Code here[133].

Article 235 has the basic statute against theft. It reads:

"A person who steals the property of another commits the crime of theft and shall be punished by imprisonment with work for not more than 10 years or a fine of not more than 500,000 yen."

There is also a special provision dealing with the theft of electricity in Article 245. Bitcoins are not electricity, but this shows how the Penal Code has reacted earlier to technology that was new at the time. That Article reads:

"With regard to the crimes prescribed under this Chapter, electricity shall be deemed to be property."

At first glance, bitcoins are a form of property and therefore stealing them should be theft under Article 235. Let's discuss this question in some detail.

---

[132] Anonymous, Crisis Strategy Draft, k-lenz.de/btc026.
[133] k-lenz.de/btc027.

b) Three possible ways of stealing bitcoins

When discussing theft of bitcoins under Japanese law, the first thing to discuss is the various ways such a theft can happen. These may very well need to be treated in different ways.

What does it mean to "own a bitcoin"? The Bitcoin protocol is a distributed ledger which works in a peer-to-peer environment without trust between the parties involved. But in contrast to a land register the Bitcoin protocol has no field for recording names. The only connection between a bitcoin and its rightful owner is the knowledge of a private key.

That "knowledge of a private key" in turn is not real knowledge. Most people owning bitcoins don't even know one private key. Instead sometimes they own pieces of paper upon which that key is printed. That is called a Bitcoin paper wallet. It contains a public address and the corresponding private key.

It is impossible to steal the private key by hacking the paper wallet. When one stores private keys on a computing device, that information may be grabbed by a third party by planting a virus or keyboard logger on that device. That is obviously impossible for a paper wallet.

For the analysis here, that leaves us with three possible ways to steal a bitcoin.

Case one is where criminal A physically removes a paper wallet from the possession of victim B. In that case, B will not have access to whatever bitcoins were stored in the address printed on that paper wallet, unless he had some kind of backup in place. But let's just assume that's not the case.

This case is not much different from stealing a $100 banknote. The main point is that in this first case the criminal removes a physical object from the control of the victim.

Of course stealing a $100 banknote is theft everywhere on the planet. Is there any relevant difference to the case where the criminal just removes a paper wallet from the physical control of the victim?

There well may be.

The value of the bitcoin paper wallet does not come from the paper involved. It comes from the information, from the ability to access the private key.

That point will become clear if one thinks of a different way to steal bitcoins from a paper wallet.

The criminal may, instead of removing the

piece of paper completely from the physical control of the victim, just take a picture of the private key with his mobile phone. That would be the second possible case.

In that case, there is no need to move the paper wallet in any way. The thief will still be able to move the bitcoins on that particular Bitcoin address to some other address he controls.

The difference to the above case, where the criminal completely removes the piece of paper from the victim's physical control is that in this case the victim still could dispose of the bitcoins stored at this Bitcoin address as long as the thief has not yet done a transaction removing them. As long as that does not happen, the victim still has his money. If by chance he just transfers his bitcoins to another address before the thief gets around to moving the bitcoins, the damage will be avoided. Which means that the damage to the property of the victim is not complete until that further step happens.

This case would be rather similar to a case decided in 1984 by the Tokyo District Court[134].

In that case, the thief took a secret file concerning the development of a new drug from the victim company, copied that secret file with a

---

[134] Tokyo District Court June 28, 1984.

photocopier, and then put the file right back where it was in the first place.

The Tokyo District Court sentenced the defendant for theft.

This is not a clear cut case of theft. The defendant in this case was not after the physical object in question, the paper upon which the information he was interested in was printed. He wanted the information. And the damage to the victim came from the fact that although the victim was still able to access this information, exclusivity had been lost.

With the development of a new drug, the damage comes from the fact that a competing company may receive a patent for the drug in question first, shutting out the victim from bringing their invention to market. This situation is similar to the case where someone takes a picture of a private key on a paper wallet with a mobile phone.

In both cases, information that was previously under the exclusive control of the victim is now accessible to both the victim and the thief.

But in the case of the Bitcoin paper wallet, the thief can empty the wallet immediately after getting control of the information. In the industrial spying case above the thieves would still need to beat the victim in a race to the patent office. And the victims may be able to convince the patent office that they had developed the invention in question first and therefore deserve to receive the patent. In contrast, Bitcoin transactions can't be reversed by any third party, a fact which makes it much more attractive for criminals to steal bitcoins than to steal some other form of property.

The third way of stealing bitcoins would be to somehow hack a computing device where the owner of these bitcoins has stored his private key. In that case, no physical object like a piece of paper is involved. This third case is purely about getting access to information.

c) Interpretation of the Japanese theft statute

In contrast to German law, the Japanese theft statute requires "stealing property". The word property is a translation of "zaibutsu (財物)". This wording is broader than the theft statute in German law.

German law only protects "chattels [135]"

---

[135] See the "Personal Property" Wikipedia article for an explanation of this technical term, en.wikipedia.org/wiki

(bewegliche Sache) in the theft statute (Article 242 Penal Code). There needs to be an object involved. Information as such is not protected[136]. That means that the German theft statute is not violated at least in case three above (hacking computing devices and accessing a private key). It would seem to be difficult also in the second case (taking a picture of a paper wallet).

One could argue that knowledge of a private key and therefore control over a Bitcoin address is "property". I would be sympathetic to such a view.

If one agrees with the Tokyo District Court decision discussed above, information can certainly be protected by the theft statute if it is incorporated in paper. If the owner of an industrial secret is protected against losing exclusivity of access to the information, the owner of a Bitcoin wallet should enjoy the same protection.

As already explained, if anything, the danger to the owner of the Bitcoin wallet is much more immediate. All the thief needs to do is to transfer the bitcoins out of the Bitcoin address in question. That doesn't take more than a couple of minutes. And that

---

/Personal_property.

[136] Franziska Boehm/Paulina Paesch, Bitcoins: Rechtliche Herausforderungen einer virtuellen Währung. Eine erste juristische Einordnung, MMR 2014, 75, 77.

transaction is not reversible.

So if the Japanese courts say that in the case of stealing information on industrial secrets the theft statute should apply, there is really no reason not to extend this reasoning to the case of taking a picture of a Bitcoin paper wallet private key (case two above).

Anyway, the first case discussed above is most certainly theft under the Japanese statute. It would also be theft under the German statute.

And, in contrast, the third way of stealing bitcoins (by hacking a computing device and gaining access to a private key) would not fall under the theft statute.

To sum up the results of my discussion of the Japanese theft statute: It depends on how bitcoins were stolen. In cases one and two discussed above, where a Bitcoin paper wallet is either stolen completely or a picture of the private key is taken, that constitutes theft. In the third case other statutes may apply.

2. Unauthorized Access

a) The Japanese Statute

The 1999 Act on Prohibition of Unauthorized

Computer Access makes it a crime to use someone else's password to access a computer online. An English translation is available at the Japanese government's law translation website[137].

Japan is a Member State of the Council of Europe Convention on Cybercrime (Budapest Convention). It signed the Convention on November 23, 2001, and ratified it on July 3, 2012[138].

That Convention[139] requires Member States to adopt such legislative and other measures as may be necessary to establish as criminal offenses under its domestic law, when committed intentionally, the access of the whole or any part of a computer system without right. A Party may require that the offense be committed by infringing security measures, with the intent of obtaining computer data or other dishonest intent, or in relation to a computer system that is connected to another computer system (Article 2).

Article 3 of the Japanese Unauthorized Access Act prohibits unauthorized access, and Article 11 provides a sanction of prison with work of up to three years or a fine of not more than one million yen

---

[137] k-lenz.de/btc028.
[138] Council of Europe, Convention on Cybercrime, k-lenz.de/btc093.
[139] Council of Europe, Convention on Cybercrime, k-lenz.de/btc094.

for violations.

Unauthorized access is defined in Article 2 Paragraph 4 like this:

"The term of 'act of unauthorized computer access' as used in this Act means any of the following:

"(i) An act of rendering a specified computer with an access control feature available for specified use that is subject to restrictions imposed by the access control feature concerned by inputting someone else's identification code associated with the access control feature concerned via a telecommunications link and thus operating the specified computer concerned (excluding such an act engaged in by the access administrator who has added the access control feature concerned and upon obtaining permission from the access administrator concerned or the authorized user to whom the identification code concerned belongs)

"(ii) An act of rendering a specified computer with an access control feature available for specified use that is subject to restrictions imposed by the access control feature concerned by inputting any information (excluding identification code) or command suitable for evading the restrictions on said specified use via a telecommunications link and thus operating the specified computer concerned

(excluding such an act engaged in by the access administrator who has added the access control feature concerned and upon obtaining permission from the access administrator concerned, the same applying in the following item)

"(iii) An act of rendering a specified computer available for specified use that is subject to restrictions imposed by the access control feature of another specified computer connected thereto via a telecommunications link by inputting any information or command suitable for evading said restrictions into this other computer via a telecommunications link and thus operating the specified computer concerned."

The terms "access administrator", "specified computer", and "specified use" used above are further defined in Article 2 Paragraph 1 like this:

"The term 'access administrator' as used in this Act means a person who manages the operation of a computer connected to a telecommunications link (hereinafter referred to as a 'specified computer') in relation to its use (limited to the kind realized via the telecommunications link concerned, hereafter referred to as 'specified use'."

That means Japan has restricted the prohibition against unauthorized access to online access. Stealing a password and accessing a computer directly is not unauthorized access under this Act.

The main question for the application in connection with the Bitcoin network is if a private key is an "identification code" under the definition above. There is another definition for that term in Article 2 Paragraph 2:

"The term 'identification code' as used in this Act means a code allocated to a person who, with regard to the specified use of a specified computer, has been granted permission from the access administrator with authority over said specified use (herein referred to as an 'authorized user') or the access administrator himself/herself (hereafter referred in this paragraph to as an 'authorized user or the like') so as to enable the access administrator concerned to identify this particular user or the like as distinguished from all other authorized users and the like. In concrete terms, it may be any of the following or a combination of any of the following and another code:

(i) A code whose content must not, according to the instructions of the access administrator concerned, be revealed to a third party without reason

(ii) A code that has been generated from an image of the whole or a part of the body of the authorized user or the like concerned or his/her voice using a method specified by the access administrator concerned

(iii) A code that has been generated from the signature of the authorized user or the like concerned using a method specified by the access administrator concerned."

Finally, the term "access control feature" is defined in Article 2 Paragraph 3 like this:

"The term 'access control feature' as used in this Act means a feature that has been added to a specified computer subject to specified use or another specified computer connected thereto via a telecommunications link by the access administrator with authority over the specified use off the specified computer concerned to automatically control said specified use. It shall be designed to remove all or part of the restrictions imposed on said specified use upon confirming a code input into the specified computer associated therewith by a person wishing to engage in said specified use is identical with the identification code associated with said specified use (including a combination of a code generated from the identification code using a method specified by the access administrator concerned and part of the identification code concerned, the same applying in items (i) and (ii) of the following paragraph."

b) Is Stealing Private Keys and Moving bitcoins "Unauthorized Access"?

The Bitcoin network and protocol is based on private keys. These may be possibly understood as "identification codes" under this Act. If so, that would for example mean that someone taking a picture of the QR code of another person's Bitcoin paper wallet and then proceeding to empty that wallet with the private key may be liable under this Act, as well as under the general Penal Code article dealing with theft.

Looking at the definitions above, there are several problems with treating Bitcoin network private keys as "identification codes".

The Act requires that the "identification codes" be allocated by an "access administrator" to identify this particular user. Bitcoin private keys are generated by their owners. They are not allocated by someone else.

That problem may be not decisive. After all, finger prints and other body parts, which are expressly recognized as "identification codes" under item (ii), are not generated by an access administrator either. They are generated by the user himself, in the process of normal development, and they are determined by the user's DNA. The "allocation" in that case means that the "access administrator" just specifies the procedure for access (reading the fingerprint information with hardware dedicated to that task). He does not specify any individual information for any individual user.

In the same way, one could see the "allocation" in the fact that the Bitcoin network recognizes the private key generated by the user as valid, without anybody else actually knowing or individually specifying that information.

The next problem would be the fact that Bitcoin network private keys don't identify users by name. The protocol doesn't provide a means for recording names of the users. On the other hand, the Bitcoin protocol does identify users by their public address. The definition above does not necessarily require attaching names. If it did, the protection of the Act would not extend to all services that require a password for access, but that allow for anonymous registration, like many webmail services.

Finally, the definition above requires an "access administrator" who sets the conditions for access. That is a problem because the Bitcoin network is based on a peer-to-peer concept with no central point of control. There is no Central Bitcoin Authority that could name someone personally responsible for deciding on the access to funds.

I am not sure that this should be a decisive argument. What matters is that for all practical purposes private keys work like passwords in enabling access to bitcoins stored at an address. The fact that the conditions for this access are not set by some individual access administrator, but instead by the majority of miners supporting the Bitcoin network and the protocol in force right now does not change anything about the way a private key enables access to individual bitcoins.

The Bitcoin network software is open source. That means that all decisions on the protocol are done in a democratic way. That fact should not disqualify private keys from receiving protection under this Act.

Once one sees private keys as "identification codes", there remains the question if using a stolen private key on the Bitcoin network would qualify as "unauthorized access".

Applying the definition above, again there are some problems with that.

For one, the definition of "unauthorized access" is aimed at the normal case where someone accesses one "specified computer". In contrast, using a stolen private key to move bitcoins is accessing the

Bitcoin network as a whole. It is open to debate as to whether that should be enough.

A case for comparison may be webmail stored in a cloud server. That case clearly should be covered by the prohibition of unauthorized access. In that case also, the user as well as the person accessing the mail account without authorization are not interested in accessing any specific computer, but interested in the content of mail messages stored on that particular server. They don't care where it is, and they also don't care if the storage is spread over several different computers.

But we are dealing with criminal law here. It is already a stretch to see Bitcoin private keys as "identification codes". I think it would go too far to ignore the requirement of accessing a "specified computer" on top of that.

So under existing law, I think that using a stolen private key to move bitcoins from an address is not "unauthorized access" under this statute. But it should be. In the future, this kind of statute should be amended with a view of protecting against unauthorized access to a peer-to-peer network in the same way as against unauthorized access to any individual "specified computer".

c) Clear Cases of Unauthorized Access

The above result does not mean that this Act is not relevant for the Bitcoin network. There are some cases where clearly unauthorized access under this Act is happening.

One would be an attack stealing bitcoins that a user has stored in an online wallet like the blockchain.info free service. That service is based on passwords. Users log in to their online wallet. Their password and their wallet identification code are "identification codes" under the Act. And they are operating a "specified computer" by logging into their accounts.

So if someone somehow finds out such a password and moves the funds from such an online wallet, they are of course liable criminally under this Act.

The same would apply for bitcoins held at the sites of online trading platforms like MtGox. It may be a bad idea to do so, since that leaves the user with the risk of the trading platform in question going out of business or running away with users' bitcoins. But at least for a short period of time, this risk can't be helped. If one buys bitcoins at an exchange, they need to be under the control of that exchange at least for a couple of minutes.

If someone knows the password of such a user and steals bitcoins from such an account, that would be another clear case of unauthorized access.

And this is the international standard for all countries that have ratified the Cybercrime Convention. The same should apply to the United States or to European Union Member States.

ABOUT THE AUTHOR

Karl-Friedrich Lenz is a Professor of German and European Law at Aoyama Gakuin University in Tokyo. He blogs about issues of climate change and energy as well as the Bitcoin network at Lenz Blog, found at k-lenz.de/1. His Twitter feed is found @Kf_Lenz.

www.ingramcontent.com/pod-product-compliance
Lightning Source LLC
Chambersburg PA
CBHW071419170526
45165CB00001B/334